Love, Learning Disabilities and Pockets of Brilliance

Love, Learning Disabilities and Pockets of Brilliance

How Practitioners Can Make a Difference to
the Lives of Children, Families and Adults

SARA RYAN

Jessica Kingsley Publishers
London and Philadelphia

First published in Great Britain in 2021 by Jessica Kingsley Publishers
An Hachette Company

1

Copyright © Sara Ryan 2021

A CIP catalogue record for this title is available from the British Library and the Library of Congress

ISBN 978 1 78775 191 0
eISBN 978 1 78775 192 7

Printed and bound in the Great Britain by Clays Ltd

Jessica Kingsley Publishers' policy is to use papers that are natural, renewable and recyclable products and made from wood grown in sustainable forests. The logging and manufacturing processes are expected to conform to the environmental regulations of the country of origin.

Jessica Kingsley Publishers
73 Collier Street
London N1 9BE, UK

www.jkp.com

Contents

Foreword by Michael Edwards 6

Foreword by Rob Mitchell and Elaine James 7

Preface 11

1. What Is 'Normal', Anyway? 17

2. A Brief Historical Whizz Through 25

3. The Early Days of Difference 43

4. Childhood Challenges and Wondrousness 63

5. Love's Labour and More 91

6. Becoming an Adult 109

7. Growing Older, Death and Dying 133

8. The Outlook: Patchy with Pockets of Brilliance 151

Endnotes 157

Subject Index 171

Author Index 175

Foreword

I left school in 1969. I went to a training centre at Wheatley. I hated it. Doing menial tasks like sorting out plastics for little money. Some of the people shouldn't have been there either. I put up with it until they started charging us to be there. This was in the 1980s. It was Thatcher's time.

I came to a satellite group in Bicester. I didn't stay there long. I got out of there and went to a meeting in Nottingham with Nottingham People First. We had a meeting on a Saturday a few years after we discussed it with a lot of people. The transport turned up and tried to make us leave early. And I said no.

Eventually I got out of the system, twiddled my thumbs for a couple of years then started My Life My Choice with three other people. That was 20 years ago. I don't have a lot to do with social services unless I need them. They are needed but if they did things properly things would not happen, things would not go wrong. When you've got a problem you need to be able to access support.

The biggest achievement I think is to get where we are now with My Life My Choice, and helping Sara with what happened with Connor. I was very proud to do that, to help her with that. I've chosen my words carefully so as not to upset her. We've still got a lot of work to do.

Michael Edwards, President, My Life My Choice, an award-winning charity run by and for people with learning disabilities www.mylifemychoice.org.uk

Foreword

We found Sara one Saturday morning on Twitter after Connor had died. She had just posted the most beautiful blog *The Footy Guy Nights* which had caught Rob's attention, being a huge football fan (and a social worker). It was filled with love. We were instantly captured and found a world filled with pockets of brilliance, the Justice Quilt, animations and videos, buses and camino walks, the 107 days campaign. We found through Sara an extraordinary celebration of life and humanity which inspired creativity in response.

We also found deep desolation, grief and unbearable pain of a level that hurt your eyes to read. Pain so bad that when Sara wrote 'howl', which was frequent, you knew it was literal. And yet, despite the most horrendous backdrop imaginable, the death of her beautiful son and the need for a mass movement of people to stand with the grieving family to demand Justice for LB, we found the most extraordinary human resolve and sheer determination not to give up on ensuring that the brilliance Connor brought into her life and her family's life would never be overwhelmed and overshadowed by the way he had been taken from her and from them. A determination not to slam the door shut on health and social care with all of her remaining energy but to instead keep on sharing that brilliance and the brilliance of other people and their families and continue to engage with us and encourage us and others like us to get to know Connor and Sara and all the other people and be part of their world is a gift that is beyond generous and altruism and is borne out of love and compassion.

As professionals working in adult social care, we recognised the casual attribution of 'other' and the associations of 'risk' conflated with 'danger' in the experiences Sara described. We recognised the language. The difficult mother. The interfering sibling. In amongst our professional discomfort, critically reflecting on why we cried when we read Sara's pain, we found resolve to ask ourselves the question - how were we 'supporting' learning disabled people? Where were we for Connor? And at Winterbourne? And at Whorlton Hall? Were we in those awful settings using the same language about family members who were asking us to help their loved one?

In a Zoom call, one ridiculously hot Thursday afternoon in May during the Covid Lockdown, we were reading to each other our favourite extracts from the book as we drafted this foreword. We once again stumbled on some words by Sara in the book that left us unable to continue that day. "Being told that we would probably need respite from our son when he reached his teens was not only a brutal statement in that moment, but also (temporarily) erased the joy, love, brilliance, knowledge, generosity and thoughtfulness that Connor would contribute to our family." The minute we read it we knew it was right. In our careers, we had both been part of similar conversations. Similar small acts of harm by omission. It was a hard jolt to see it in black and white. The honest brutality of what respite really is from a family's perspective. We also can hear the, hopefully, well-meaning health and social care practitioner saying the phrase without critical thought about the layers of meaning in those words. It might have been said to help prepare, out of genuine concern, an offer made to alleviate the pressure of the perceived need to act and do something that makes the worker feel better, that they have 'helped'. But it gets everything wrong. In one statement it captures all the risk to the person and the life they could lead or will lead. When what the social worker says and what the family hears are so far apart that all the love and humanity are reduced to a menu of services in which one size fits all.

So, we feel this book should be the most precious manual for health and social care staff that there is. It will teach you more in a single chapter which reflects love and hope and uniqueness than any other core text than you can hope to find.

This book helps us as practitioners to begin to address them because wrapped up in stories of love, and compassion, and humour, and hope, are deep rooted and pointed challenges that when we read them connect with our shared humanity, reducing us to tears, making us physically wince with pain and making us laugh out loud in joy and happiness.

This book should become a seminal work, central to all social work training. It breaks through the conversation about "difficult families". The occupational stress to social workers of putting the call off to the arsy family member, is the life of the person living day by day by day. If you are not in alliance with families, to the point where you become an accomplice in their fight for the rights of their child, then you are in a parallel professional world that isn't social care and won't make a difference in people's lives.

That Sara still has the willingness and determination to work with professionals, sharing her families most intimate and private lives in order to encourage our reflection on our purpose and role and contribution is a testament to her love for Connor. How she has the patience to do so is something we can only watch and read with astonished respect. That she has managed to channel all that went before into a book that takes the reader on a beautiful journey of hope and good practice, from pre-birth through to old age and death, whilst drawing on experiences that left Sara and others so desolate and broken, is a work of art in its in it's own right.

So we end with Sara's question "what are the fundamental questions that social workers and social work students need to know about our families?" and conclude that the answer, in fact, is perfectly illustrated throughout this wonderful book. We do indeed need to know that we are all human and that this book celebrates the full extent of the brilliance of humanity in all its forms and we are forever grateful.

Rob Mitchell, Principal Worker and Elaine James, Learning Disabilities Commissioner

Preface

Introducing me and my family

This is a book that aims to celebrate and underline the humanity of people, and to share experiences of what good care and support can look like for families, learning-disabled children and adults.

It's a book about people. One set of people who feature throughout are me and my family, so before we set off on this rip-roaring read (yes, really), I will provide a brief background to my family.

So, I'm a mother, partner, daughter, sister, aunt, niece, cousin, mate, campaigner and social scientist, which is quite a list.

Rich, a political scientist and criminologist, and I live in an Oxford suburb on the route of the Oxford Tube coach service to London. Our children are Rosie (26), Will (26), Connor (still 18), Owen (23) and Tom (20). The growing-up years with five children were, with hindsight, reminiscent of an American comedy drama as the kids stumbled, bumbled, shouted, laughed, cried, raged and fell over each other and their friends in our tatty and stuff-filled house and with their extended families. Chaotic with additional layers and challenges introduced by having to deal with the detritus that comes with having a disabled child at the tail end of the 20th century.

Connor received his first diagnostic label during my undergraduate sociology and anthropology degree at Oxford Brookes University around 1996. Once I'd managed to get out of bed after a few days of despair, and back to studying, I began to focus wherever possible on disability, in particular learning disability and autism. My academic life followed a path shaped by my experiences with Connor, including a doctorate at Warwick University exploring mothers' experiences of going out in public spaces with their learning-disabled and/or autistic children.

We muddled through fairly well until Connor, also known as Laughing Boy or LB, approached 18 and began his second year in the sixth form of a 'special' unit attached to a large comprehensive school about five miles from where we live. Connor was diagnosed with autism, learning disabilities and, later, epilepsy. He attended this school from the age of four, and spent 14 years mostly contented and happy with his classmates and a set of teaching assistants and teachers who generated a person-centred education without naming it as anything so fancy.

School staff played quite a key role in Connor's experiences of epilepsy. This kicked in when he was around 15. They witnessed various seizures, and his school diary* became a source of information exchange around whether or not he appeared to be a bit out of sorts, clammy or distracted during the day. This was in marked contrast to the attention paid by health professionals.

In the period leading up to his 18th birthday in November 2012, Connor became unpredictable and deeply unhappy. School again played a central role in trying to pin down what was happening and why. There was no other support available, and after some tense and sometimes terrifying months and reluctant school exclusions, I was told about a specialist NHS assessment and treatment unit about two miles from home.

We had attended the odd psychiatric-related appointment on the same site over the years without knowing the unit existed. On 19 March 2013 we had Connor admitted to the unit for what we thought would be a few weeks of assessment and treatment with a large specialist staff and only five patients. Connor was sectioned that first night and restrained, face down, for over ten minutes (my fingers ache typing these words and my heart howls). He had never so much as sat on a naughty step before that night.

One hundred and seven days later, on 4 July 2013, on a baking-

---

* I've included some of these diary extracts throughout the book to add a sprinkling of ordinariness and fun.

hot morning, Connor drowned in the bath while staff did a Tesco online food order about eight feet away. A gentle, curious, hilarious and generous young man who loved his family, our dog Chunky Stan, London buses, lorries, classic British comedies and justice. My account of his life, his death and our subsequent campaigning for justice is captured in *Justice for Laughing Boy*[1] and on my blog 'MyDaftLife'* – named and created two years before events took such a catastrophic turn.

We faced a gruelling fight for accountability in our state of utter devastation. In short, the NHS Trust responsible took a now familiar – though, at the time, shocking – route of stating that Connor died of natural causes and tried to shut down meaningful investigation into his death. This led to a gargantuan battle in which countless members of the public from diverse backgrounds stood up alongside us in what became a social movement called #JusticeforLB.

Over the next five years, the campaign generated laughter, colour and joy, raised awareness and maintained a steady, sometimes sweary path, overcoming obstacle after obstacle placed in front of us by well-oiled state machinery. An important strand in our attempt to get answers and accountability were human rights specialists. Early intervention by a barrister, Caoilfhionn Gallagher, who was following my blog, put us in touch with the charity INQUEST; and by the time the NHS Trust published board minutes a few weeks after Connor's death, effectively stating 'nothing to see here', we had probably one of the strongest legal teams possible ahead of Connor's inquest.

#JusticeforLB raised the £25,000 needed to be represented at an inquest (excluding the pro-bono support we were given) through selling postcards of Connor's artwork and other fundraising activities. A travesty of a so-called justice system as state bodies draw on the public purse, arming themselves to the hilt with solicitors, barristers and others. We pushed for and endured a police investigation, two independent investigations

---

* https://mydaftlife.com

by a company called Verita, a ten-day inquest and a General Medical Council disciplinary tribunal. The NHS Trust referred six nurses to the Nursing and Midwifery Council, but we gave that a swerve as it seemed inappropriate to blame frontline staff for what turned out to be broader failings in leadership. Finally, in March 2018, the Trust pleaded guilty in a Health and Safety Executive criminal prosecution for Connor's death and that of a second patient, Teresa Colvin, and was fined £2 million – the biggest fine in the history of the NHS.

This was a time of immense sadness, distress, anxiety and anger, as we became almost vigilantes in seeking accountability. We were able to draw on a range of expertise across various fields and on humanness, as dirty trick after dirty trick was played: documents withheld and delayed; lies circulated; slurs launched most commonly at a 'mum' who worked full-time so was not able to look after her child. #JusticeforLB generated an antidote to this darkness with a creative, colourful and joyful productivity covering diverse terrain. This is documented in my first book and it is impossible to identify highlights given that every single contribution was, in its own way, magical.*

Indeed, our campaign #JusticeforLB and other family- and ally-led campaigns such as #Rightfulives† and #FliptheNarrative‡ have had more impact in some ways, as they remain grounded and outside of the formulaic, bureaucratic, too often sterile and jargon-drenched circles which cloak these scandals and deny them air, coherence, action, spontaneity and brilliance. These grassroots campaigns typically run with no funding, no agenda other than change and accountability, and little or no structure. #JusticeforLB also seems to have influenced individual practice, given the number of emails, messages and more we have received from health and social care students and professionals. Indeed, a recent cheeky cuppa with an ex-health minister revealed that

---

* The contributions are laid out in full colour here: https://107daysofaction.wordpress.com
† https://rightfullives.net
‡ https://candoella.com/lets-flipthenarrative

NHS-related reforms were implemented on the back of the scandal generated by Connor's death.

Through my blog, Connor was a fully fleshed-out and appealing young man who gained a wide audience of followers. The funny stories caught people's attention and they responded to him accordingly, again underlining the importance of this book. Our claims for change have to remain measured, however, as in the past few years there has been a steady drip of heart-breaking stories about the unspeakable treatment of people that has led to death or serious harm.

About this book

After writing *Justice for Laughing Boy*, I wanted to write a book that generates further insight and understanding into the lives of learning-disabled people and their families.

To generate a space free from jargon and empty concepts, from the constraints and weight of 'official' processes and discourses – a space in which the love, laughter and joy that is woven through families such as ours can shine through, alongside the challenges.

We know so much about what support and services should look like in order to enable flourishing lives, and yet our lives as families too often remain beleaguered and invisible. I've taken a chronological approach, realizing in the process how it becomes harder to mine the drops of brilliance as people grow older.

The book has been a beast to write. I have alternated between wanting to lob the manuscript into the nearest skip and thinking 'Get in! This is so needed.' All the while feeling quiet despair that we still need to rake over this stuff to try to rehumanize a loosely linked group of people and their families who are too often stripped of personhood, care, dignity and respect.

I was asked by a friend early on if I was writing a textbook or memoir. A textbook involves a drier style, bullets and action points. For me, this is a mixed memoir: a collection of stories and experiences with the odd set of bullet points where appropriate.

In writing it, I have drawn on a bundle of personal experiences, research interviews and informal chats with learning-disabled and/or autistic people, families, health and social care professionals,[*] academic research, policy documents, tweets, podcasts, fiction and autobiographies.

This includes research funded by the Wellcome Trust that I was privileged to have carried out ten years ago in a project exploring the experiences of parents of autistic children, and later extended to include autistic people, grandparents and siblings.[†] Lay summaries of the findings are published on Healthtalk.org.[‡]

From academia, I draw on extensive research on how to improve the lives and wellbeing of learning-disabled and/or autistic people. This has consistently demonstrated both what is important to people and the repeated failures of services to achieve this.

Indeed, there must be warehouses full of research evidence that learning-disabled people draw a short straw in pretty much every aspect of life.[2] Life expectancy is substantially lower[3] and less than 6% of people are in paid employment.[4] People are likely to have limited friendships,[5] and sexual relationships can be limited or prevented.[6] Just listing these points makes my heart feel heavy and generates queasiness in my stomach. Limited friendships and prevented sexual relationships...

From this evidence we know what we need to know, and it isn't complicated or even tricky. Love, relationships, effective support and community engagement are as important to learning-disabled people as they are to pretty much everyone in the UK and wider. Instead, we have 'independent supported living' as a thing underpinned by an over-emphasis on rights, independence and choice that is not translating into good lives.[7] There remains so much room for improvement, so much room for doing things

---

[*]   I'm including everyone who works with learning-disabled and/or autistic people under 'professionals'. In our experience, some of the most professional practice has been demonstrated by support workers and students.

[†]   A second researcher, Dr Anne-Marie Boylan, conducted the sibling and grandparent interviews.

[‡]   https://healthtalk.org/parents-children-autism-spectrum/overview. Descriptions of the children are here: https://healthtalk.org/parents-children-autism-spectrum/the-children

differently and better, and yet the pace of change remains glacial. A smorgasbord of inertia.

This devastating roll call is despite a solid raft of policies over the last few decades aiming to improve people's lives.

These sources all feed into this book, and I remain indebted to the people who have given up their time and shared their stories and experiences so freely with me.

From these strands, I've attempted to weave a comprehensive, colourful and compelling picture of families with learning-disabled and/or autistic children and adults in the UK.

Where are we now?

I have a now-yellowed-round-the-edges copy of Helen Featherstone's *A Difference in the Family: Life with a Disabled Child*,[8] written 40 years ago.

I bought it in 2001, desperate to absorb knowledge and understanding to help me make sense of what family life is like when a child is disabled. I read it in the days when I still thought writing on book pages was almost sinful, so the book is in pristine condition with the odd imprint of a corner temporarily turned. At the bottom of page 3 are the words:

> Actually, it hardly matters how we label these people. Their limitations will touch the lives of their sisters and brothers, their mothers and fathers. The troubles and pleasures of these families are my subject.

Oof. What a statement.

I'd like to think that my younger self, floundering in a space of newness, confusion, devastation and puzzlement, and with retrospective permission to write all over text, would have vigorously underlined the words 'these people' and 'their limitations', and peppered the margin with exclamation marks.

I know I would not have. It would take a good year or so before I was able to begin to recognize that our son was not the problem in this new world our family had entered; that his 'limitations' were constructed and sustained by a tyrannical and punitive regime which worked to erase any consideration of his kick-ass and uncompromising brilliance. An example of disablism defined by Dan Goodley as 'the oppressive practices of contemporary society that threaten to exclude, eradicate and neutralise those individuals, bodies, minds and communicative practices that fail to fit the capitalist imperative'.[9] In short: fit in, be productive (in a narrowly defined way), or off you pop.

While Featherstone's book, which was at the time considered to be a 'wise, compassionate account' (as stated on the cover), is clearly outdated, the sentiment remains consistent. Family life with disabled children remains externally coated in burden and troublesomeness, and parents continue to make concerted attempts to generate space for family members to be recognized as fully human and valued.

People remain marginalized, living in residential settings or in houses in the community with such low levels of support that they may rarely have the opportunity to go out and join in with mainstream activities.

Children tend to be educated in specialist schools (if not excluded), bussed to and from these institutions on 'special transport', removing the opportunity for parents to get to know each other and children to muck in and just get on with difference and diversity.

Families are differentially positioned in terms of intersectional factors such as ethnicity, social class and sexuality, and yet we share broadly similar experiences of marginalization with different-sized mountains to scale and varying access to tools to do so.

We have few mechanisms to capture the ordinary, everyday stuff, while circulation of sensationalist tropes around 'warrior mums' and 'heroic kids' acts to further pathologize* and marginalize people through the process of singling them out and badging them as 'other'. This is worsened by research agendas underpinned by

---

* That is, to make out the person is somehow abnormal, that there is something wrong with them.

negativity and gross assumptions about our lives, generating research findings that bear little resemblance to our experiences.

Barriers to a good life can be reinforced by health and social care professionals who too often operate within a medicalized arena. The problem or deficit is laid firmly at the child's feet (or sometimes their 'errant' mother, less commonly father) rather than the ways in which society is organized.

Decades of activist and academic work in the disability community establishing different models of disability and impairment, have not quite entered the worlds of health and social care in a sustained way when it comes to learning disability and autism. We remain generally ill-equipped to embrace diversity, despite legislative changes such as the Equality Act 2010.

This 'deficit model' is also on display each autumn with the annual Children in Need telethon. Disabled and other marginalized children are depicted as 'in need' and to be pitied alongside a mawkish wounded yellow bear 'mascot'. 'Charity porn', as disabled photographer and writer David Hevey described it back in the day: charity advertising as 'the visual flagship for the myth of the tragedy of impairment'.[10] This event has run for nearly 40 years now, raising an extraordinary amount of money, despite little substantive change in the situation of the children it claims to support and their families in the UK.

The landscape of learning disability and autistic provision has shifted a bit. Many people in the UK will have heard of Winterbourne View, where staff in a privately run assessment and treatment unit in Bristol were exposed to be brutalizing patients in 2011. The *Panorama* documentary *Undercover Care: The Abuse Exposed*[*] generated a public outcry and a flurry of (what turned out to be) limited measures to move patients out of these places and back into their own homes. A scandal was born and then faltered, despite the riches and reach of big charities, third-sector organizations and institutions, and much standing up loudly to support various iterations of work that slowly fizzled away.

---

* www.bbc.co.uk/blogs/panorama/2011/05/undercover_care_the_abuse_expo.html

It remains baffling how some people are subjected to inhumane treatment without apparent action (rather than empty words) and little sustained interest. Indeed, a new *Panorama* undercover investigation[*] into another privately run assessment and treatment unit, Whorlton Hall near Durham, included similarly grotesque footage of patients being abused, tortured and taunted. It barely generated a ripple across the UK in May 2019.

---

[*] www.bbc.co.uk/iplayer/episode/m00059qb/panorama-undercover-hospital-abuse

Chapter 1

What Is 'Normal', Anyway?

This book could be a very short book: what do health and social care professionals and students need to know about our families?

The answer is: *we are all human.*

It is really that simple. Chris Goodey, a UK academic in intellectual history, develops this argument further by suggesting that learning disabilities (and autism) emerge through an 'inclusion phobia' felt by the mainstream population:

> The idea that everyone means everyone does not amount to holding a position at all. It goes without saying. It does not require justification. People are people. A position is only taken by someone who feels like drawing boundaries.[1]

By identifying and pointing out certain people as learning disabled and/or autistic, we are moving away from a society where *everyone* is considered to be human. We draw boundaries because we need to identify learning-disabled and/or autistic children, adults and their families in order to explore their experiences and learn to do better for all of us.

I borrow here from a classic text that the influential American sociologist Erving Goffman wrote on stigma.[2] Setting aside consideration of the merit of stigma as a concept, Goffman identified two categories of 'sympathetic others' in people's lives. Sympathetic others are those ready to adopt the standpoint of the person and share with them the feeling that they are human and 'essentially normal'.

'The own' are those with intimate knowledge of the experience of those perceived to be stigmatized – so, in this instance, 'the own' refers to learning-disabled and/or autistic people.

'The wise' are those who find themselves accorded a measure of acceptance, a measure of courtesy membership, which could include health or social care professionals who have developed rich insight into people's experiences or family members. Goffman suggests that 'the wise' may go through a 'heart-changing personal experience'[3] to reach this status and provide a model of 'normalization' for how far other people should treat the person as if they did not have a stigmatized identity.

The concept of 'the wise' is important here because one of the key issues for families with disabled children is that there can be no or very little previous experience of disability. My knowledge, understanding and experience of disability until my son Connor's diagnosis was pretty thin and anecdotal.

My mum was involved in a Brownie pack with disabled children, so, as children, we went inside the gates of Buckingham Palace for a Changing-of-the-Guard gig. That was about it really. Brief, almost exotic experiences, slight brushes with difference sitting outside what was then a reassuringly familiar and recognizable world.

There is some irony that, a couple of decades on from the Buckingham Palace event, as our family manoeuvred its way around supermarkets, town centres and seasides, the act of catching the rare eye of another parent of a disabled child was deeply reassuring. We were not alone on this journey with few signposts and little apparent support. There were *familiar others*.

When our children are edged outside of textbook definitions of 'normal', we enter a new space with a new language and a range of professionals to engage with. Early on in this process we grasp on to whatever we can with a naive and understandable blinkered hopefulness that initially propels us to try to 'fix something'.[4]

Jessie Hewitson, journalist and author of *Autism: How to Raise a Happy Autistic Child*,[5] was a guest on the '1800 Seconds of Autism' podcast* in 2019. The presenters asked her what she felt

---

* www.bbc.co.uk/programmes/p06sdq0x/episodes/downloads

about her son's diagnosis. Her careful and sensitive reflections about how she was thrown by the diagnosis because of a lack of knowledge about autism were moving. She could now clearly see how attempts to impose 'normal' activities on her son, such as repeatedly taking him to 'one of those godawful music groups for babies and toddlers', caused him considerable distress. I hold my hand up for this type of attempted normalization activity and suspect many parents would.

It is almost impossible not to, really, as we are consistently fed normative beliefs and assumptions about disability being something awful and dreaded. We are disablist through ignorance and this is magnified almost during the process of becoming and being pregnant, giving birth and in interactions with healthcare professionals, family, friends and other parents at baby and toddler groups.

In my life, instead of celebrating and enjoying the peacefulness and curiosity that Connor exuded, I initially perceived it as somehow wrong or problematic. I would not have pulled up Featherstone writing about limited people in 2001. However, eventually comes a form of enlightenment and an accompanying shift to becoming 'wise'.

A few years later, I barely noticed when I found Connor in the kitchen, in the swing bin.

Retreating to the empty bin after a busy school day offered him a slightly separate space of calm security while the afternoon activities of cooking, clearing up, homework and sorting stuff out was going on. I recognized that, after a full-on day of liveliness, noise, bright lights and activity, plus a good one-hour journey on a bus to and from school, it made sense to seek a place of quiet containment.

As a parent of young children, having one happily stowed in a bin when I made tea was also a kind of win. My only concern was a slight worry about what would happen if a health or social care professional unexpectedly pitched up.

As with parents, how professionals become 'wise' should be a key goal in being and remaining an effective and reflective practitioner. Co-mingling is always a good strategy: hanging out with learning-disabled and/or autistic children and adults. This can be face to face, virtually or by reading.

For example, getting involved with local self-advocacy or carer groups, following learning-disabled and/or autistic people on Twitter or reading autobiographies like *Spectrum Women*,[6] *Odd Girl Out*[7] and *Nerdy, Shy, and Socially Inappropriate: A User Guide to an Asperger Life*.[8] Hashtags like #ActuallyAutistic offer invaluable nugget-sized insights into people's everyday lives, experiences and perspectives.

Pockets of brilliance – professionals who work with children, families and adults

In summer 2019 I tweeted asking families to provide examples of 'sparkling actions' by health or social care professionals. The response was overwhelming, and I will weave these tweets throughout the book. Most were about health care professionals; a second nudge for examples related to social care generated but a handful of responses, which may be a point worth reflecting on – perhaps a rallying call for positive action?

Dr 'Dr' Sara Ryan
@sarasiobhan

Desperately seeking examples of sparkling actions (big or small) by health/social care peeps for families with learning disabled/autistic children. [thanks] #Book2 #Magic

7:59 PM · Jul 30, 2019 · Twitter Web App

Shortly after this Twitter flurry I attended a #BrewEd* event in Reading. #BrewEd is a grassroots movement of educators (and others) who get together for events in pubs and drink while

---

*   www.tes.com/news/meet-men-bringing-pub-based-cpd-nation

discussing serious issues around disability. Strangely, it works brilliantly.

Two parents, Emma and Helen, gave a talk about their experiences of health care for their children. Helen has two sons with complex health needs. She broke down when recounting her first meeting with the community nurse ten years ago who said she knew nothing about Helen's older son's condition but she would learn. In the break, Helen said that the strength of emotion she experienced recalling that conversation was unexpected. The impact of experiencing excellent practice runs long and deep.

The responses to the Twitter request raised similar recollections of what are tiny actions, sometimes from years ago, that remain powerfully memorable.

Katherine Runswick-Cole, a mother, scholar and activist, tweeted during this exchange that she was reminded of the literature from critical race theory about micro-aggressions – unconscious or subtle forms of pervasive racism.

She likened the sparkling tweets to micro-kindnesses in a sea of micro- and macro-aggressions. This is why they matter so much. As I will demonstrate throughout this book, families can experience unconscious or subtle forms of pervasive disablism which can have considerable impact. The tweets describe often tiny shifts in practice which counteract or soothe this.

The Twitter thread also generated discussion about how families were contributing examples that should not be considered 'sparkling', but were instead simply examples of professionals doing their jobs well. For example, taking into account the whole family rather than treating the child as an 'atomized' individual – a separate person who has little contact with others. I agree these actions should not be considered 'sparkling'; however, in a health and social care system that consistently fails certain groups of people, they are worthy of flagging up. If nothing else, highlighting what makes a difference to families can generate insights into how professionals can make small shifts in their practice to better support families.

One exchange during this exercise speaks to Helen's point

about genuine engagement and inclusion phobia, and brings us back to Goffman's idea of 'the wise':

> Often find that people who have not yet been indoctrinated into low expectation culture of LD/SEND have more sparkle. But dread hearing 'don't worry love, I've worked with them before'. There is no them, only people. (Katherine Runswick-Cole – @K_Runswick_Cole)

> 'We've had one of them before' sent me running, weeping from one secondary school. I settled for the honesty of 'this is all new for us but we'll be led by you!' (Liz Wilson – @ hillsideliz)

The direction of 'travel' in terms of professional practice – whether you are a support worker, social worker, nurse, health professional, commissioner and so on – should be towards improving. Always trying to do better. In the field of support for learning-disabled and/or autistic people, a malaise seems to contaminate good practice, as the above tweets suggest.

We will see in the following chapter historical evidence of a consistent drag that means we never get beyond consideration of 'them' and 'us'.

Love, finally

Love is a central feature of family life and yet remains invisible in health and social care services, practice and research. Where is the love? And why is this word erased in the professional arena? Not scientific enough perhaps, or too messy to engage with?

It may be that thinking about love is too uncomfortable for professionals; although Chloe Silverman, a Science, Technology and Society academic, argues the emotional work of science becomes visible when professionals and parents interact in consultations, suggesting a mutual interdependence between love and science.[9]

Recognizing the love in families would surely put a bit of a halt on some of the negative practices that continue to thrive, and allow a better understanding among professionals of the actions we take.

Whatever the reasons for this omission, examples of sparkling practice underpinned by love, thoughtfulness and care will be sprinkled throughout this book.

I hope readers will come to it with an open mind and an open heart, embrace the challenges and trickiness it offers, recognize the love that underpins it and ultimately enjoy it!

Chapter 2

A Brief Historical Whizz Through

This brief summary of the historical context will act as a soft mattress from which to make sense of the rest of the book. This history has been written in solid and brilliant scholarly detail by others (I recommend *From Idiocy to Mental Deficiency: Historical Perspectives on People with Learning Disabilities* by Anne Digby and David Wright[1] and *Neurotribes: The Legacy of Autism and How to Think Smarter about People Who Think Differently* by Steve Silberman[2] as good starting points), so my aim here is to present a potted history, picking up on salient and sometimes quirky points. On being human.

In the 18th century, enlightenment and the accompanying processes of industrialization led to a shift from traditional authority based on religion to rational, scientific thinking. The move from rural settings to the development of large, intense spaces of urbanization both generated and highlighted a raft of social problems which included poverty, health, hygiene and literacy.

It also led to the identification of certain people who were not able to work in this transformed space and became a 'social issue'. This group included single mothers, 'drunks' and other 'reprobate' characters as well as disabled adults and children. Concern about this issue was initially framed in terms of thinking about how to help children and adults learn to undertake some sort of paid employment or trade – in effect, to enable and support people to become productive members of society.

The beginnings of institutionalization

In 1847 the setting up of the Charity for the Asylum of Idiots led to the development of large long-stay institutions and the incarceration of children and adults in 'colonies' typically based outside cities. People were removed from society. We do not have to look far to see that current institutions – the assessment and treatment units – remain on the edges of towns and cities.

The first asylum based in Highgate, London, moved to a purpose-built building in Surrey in 1855. The Royal Earlswood Hospital could accommodate 400 people (mostly children) in 15-bedded dormitories. It extended to 800 beds in the 1870s and the largely self-sufficient site included a farm and 50 acres of pleasure gardens. 'Inmates' were encouraged to learn trades such as carpentry or bookmaking to help them when they rejoined society. The institution went through various changes across the 20th century until it closed on 31 March 1997 amid allegations of abuse. The whiff of abuse is never far from these places. In 2011, it emerged that two of the Queen's cousins, Nerissa and Katherine Bowes-Lyons, lived in the hospital from the ages of 15 and 22. Nerissa died in 1986 aged 66, and Katherine died in 2014 aged 87. Once news broke, the royal family replaced the plastic name tag and serial number marking Nerissa's grave with a gravestone.

The Idiots Act (1886) differentiated between people labelled as 'lunatics' (people with mental ill health) and 'imbeciles' (learning-disabled people). Early on in the 20th century, the Eugenics Education Society was set up and supported by notable and influential people, including Virginia Woolf, George Bernard Shaw and H.G. Wells.[3] Considerable concern had grown about the 'fitness' of society, and early intentions to educate were replaced with a determination to raise the fertility levels of those deemed to be superior. People classed as 'idiots' and 'imbeciles' were held to be rampantly promiscuous.[*]

---

[*] The Wellcome Library has a comprehensive, digital archive of the Eugenics Education Society which is worth a browse to get an idea of the horror promulgated around learning disability, shades of which remain today: https://wellcomelibrary.org/collections/digital-collections/makers-of-modern-genetics/digitised-archives/eugenics-society

A Report by the Royal Commission on Care and Control of the Feebleminded (1908) recommended a 'board of control', and this was set up five years later via the Mental Deficiency Act 1913. The Board of Control for Lunacy and Mental Deficiency was to oversee what had now become four categories of people: idiots, imbeciles, feeble-minded persons and moral imbeciles. (I know, keep up...)

There then followed decades of shifting labels and definitions which included 'idiot', 'imbecile', 'feeble-minded', 'moral imbecile' and 'moral defective', all with a backdrop of the eugenics movement which, among other things, pushed for compulsory sterilization to prevent certain people from reproducing. It also tried to encourage those with 'good genes' to have more children. This remains a very much contemporary strand in the UK. Toby Young, journalist and free schools campaigner, for example, was in the news after attending the London Conference on Intelligence which supports the idea of progressive eugenics.[4]

The National Health Service (NHS) and framework for the Welfare State were established in 1948; community care policies began to emerge, and terms such as 'backward', 'subnormal' and 'severely subnormal' entered the English language.

You can see persistent attempts here to categorize and redefine certain types of people more finely, as the jumble of low-regarded people that initially emerged during early industrialization, including single mothers and alcoholics, was stripped away in line with eugenic thinking. Primacy was attached to the idea of intellect and 'intelligence' (shudder). After the battering of two World Wars, fears around weakened national 'stock' were rife, and moves in Germany to eradicate 'useless eaters' were not condemned by the British establishment. Indeed, University College London has long been the home of UK eugenic activity, with Francis Galton and others conducting eugenic-related research there.* Segregated long-stay hospitals for the 'mentally subnormal' became mechanisms of control and containment.

The (apparent) demise of long-stay hospitals

In 1967, the scandal of Ely Hospital for learning-disabled people unfolded, leading to what is considered to be the first NHS public inquiry. This inquiry, chaired by Geoffrey Howe, led to the creation of the hospital inspectorate which was to later become the Care Quality Commission (CQC).

What is particularly important about this scandal is that commissioning of the inquiry was an outcome of public condemnation at coverage of the abuse in the *News of the World*. A nursing assistant, Mr Pantilledes, who worked at the hospital for just over 12 months, wrote to the newspaper detailing the abuse he had witnessed after official reporting channels came to nothing. Mr Pantilledes was a health inspector from Cyprus who was unable to get a higher-grade job at the time. Mark Drakeford, a Welsh Assembly Member, chillingly said it took 'fresh eyes' to actually recognize the abuse that was taking place.[5] The inquiry was held privately, but the findings were so critical that Howe insisted that the full report be published. It is grimly fascinating and depressing that this inquiry led to major changes in the wider organization of health services and regulation, while the abuse of patients that it uncovered continues to this day.

An online resource† including interviews with a past patient, staff and other figures involved in Ely Hospital is well worth a graze to get an insight into the hospital setting. For a wider perspective of long-stay hospitals at the same time, I'd recommend sourcing a copy of Pauline Morris's book *Put Away* published in 1969.[6] Funded by Mencap (in the days when they used their time and

---

* In 2020, after a strong campaign by students and others, UCL announced a series of measures which include new scholarships to study race and racism and potentially re-naming buildings, to acknowledge and recognise the link between the university and eugenic research activity. https://www.ucl.ac.uk/news/2020/feb/ucl-announces-action-acknowledge-and-address-historical-links-eugenics
† www.peoplescollection.wales/collections/579951

resources more effectively*), Morris and her research team spent one to two weeks in half of the long-stay hospitals in England over a period of two years. Her description of aspects of everyday life is compelling, while the study also brushes over any abuse. Along with some brighter aspects, Morris captures the misery of these settings, describing 80–100-bed dormitories for children with no personal belongings, bookshelves or pictures, as well as differences that existed between the institutions in terms of care, interest and neglect. It is an extraordinary read. Peter Townsend, a sociologist, wrote in the foreword:

> A depressing picture emerges from the national survey. There is considerable personal, environmental, occupational and social deprivation among the hospital population and no good purpose can be served by concealing this fact.[7]

Again. We knew. People knew 50 years ago.

The Education (Handicapped Children) Act 1970 made education universal for the first time, and social service departments were set up in local authorities to assume responsibility for health and social services. The shift to community living was precipitated by a White Paper *Better Services for Mentally Handicapped* in 1971, and a decade later the Education Act 1981 stated that children should be educated in mainstream provision wherever possible. A year later an influential report *An Ordinary Life*, promoting the principle of people living ordinary lives, in ordinary houses, in ordinary streets, was published by the King's Fund.[8]

1981 was also the year that the *Silent Minority* documentary made by Nigel Evans aired on ATV in June. This was an account of six months spent in two long-stay hospitals: Borocourt Hospital near Reading and St Lawrence's Hospital in Caterham, Surrey. Evans seems to have been an extraordinary documentary filmmaker. *Silent Minority*† is a thoughtful, measured, insightful,

---

*   www.learningdisabilityengland.org.uk/news/a-statement-following-the-inquest-into-
      dannys-death
†   *The Silent Minority*. Accessed on 10/2/2020 at www.youtube.com/watch?v=7Qb424HvKSQ

respectful romp, almost, around these two long-stay institutions. Patients offer commentary in a humorous and human way throughout the film. One patient, sitting on a bench with a mate, watching life go past outside the institution, said, 'After all is said and done, this place is not everyone's cup of tea.'

'We live with each other and watch each other get old,' he continued, as greying photos of young boys and their much older selves were shown.

An extract from medical notes appeared on the screen:

High grade imbecile; conduct good; habits clean; works in ward.

The commentary continued:

Some people were a bit stroppy when they first came but they settle down in the end after a little bit of treatment. [...] But I often wonder why? Why they put you in and just ignore you, like honestly we're being put away.

The insights offered by these reflections are gut-wrenchingly powerful when you see the way in which people were treated, largely dismissed and overlooked. At one point, Terry Green who was in his late 50s, was filmed sitting in a wheelchair. A nurse noticed he seemed to be trying to reach for the wheel. A different chair was found with wheels that Terry could reach and he tentatively started to move forward. Evans' quietly spoken commentary:

After 40 years in bed, ten years on a bean bag, Terry Green takes his first inching steps towards independence. For decades, the full panoply of the medical profession has trooped through this ward and nobody had the wit, the initiative or imagination to give Terry this opportunity. This kind of neglect invites a whole new definition of the phrase 'mental handicap'.

There was an almost inevitable backlash when the film aired. The then Secretary of State for Social Services, Norman Fowler, said it presented an unrepresentative picture by focusing on 'certain categories of the more severely handicapped'. I know. What does this even mean? The two district health authorities (pre-NHS Trust days) involved were also indignant, accusing Evans of not following the agreed rules in making the documentary. He remained unrepentant and said it was in the interests of the British public to understand what was happening in these long-stay institutions. One of the authorities argued that a nurse was present in the outside wire cage that patients were kept in during the daytime, a statement again speaking to what was considered to be acceptable care.

Back to the policy stuff...

In 1989 a *Caring for People* White Paper[9] set out principles for the shift to community care, and long-stay hospitals began to close. In this decade the term 'people with learning difficulties' was adopted by self-advocacy groups. It is important to highlight that these changes were happening alongside the development of the wider disability movement and the emergence of Disability Studies as a discipline. The disability movement in the UK initially largely involved physically disabled people and was dominated for some time by white men.

Entering the 21st century, we see what really should have been landmark policies with *Valuing People* (2001)[10] bringing the principles of rights, independence, choice and inclusion to the fore. Individual budgets were introduced in 2007. A louder focus on the premature and preventable deaths of learning-disabled people also emerged with *Death by Indifference*, a Mencap report published in 2007.[11] This generated Jonathan Michael's equally damning *Healthcare for All: The Independent Inquiry into Access to Healthcare for People with Learning Disabilities*,[12] published the following year. The turgidity of embedded poor practice and treatment is illustrated by the publication of *Valuing People Now* in 2009,[13] urging more rapid implementation of the principles of *Valuing People* (eight long years later). Despite good intentions, a solid research evidence base involving key academic figures in the field of learning disability, such as Jack Tizard, Jim Mansell,

Jan Walmsley, Eric Emerson and many more, solid policy developments and recognition of impoverished lives, there was little change.

Death and dying

This whistle-stop tour takes us to March 2013 and publication of the *Confidential Inquiry into the Premature Deaths of People with Learning Disabilities* (CIPOLD).[14] This report identified harrowing differences in the mortality rates of learning-disabled people compared with the mainstream population. It produced 18 recommendations which included the establishment of a National Mortality Review Board to provide necessary scrutiny to understand why these deaths were happening. The government responded to this review in July 2013,[15] stating that the costs and benefits of such a review board needed weighing up (and concluding that it was too expensive to implement). Instead, the Bristol University team that undertook the CIPOLD review was commissioned to develop a 'review function'. This has become known as LeDeR. Mystery continues to shroud what this acronym stands for. Three annual LeDeR reviews[16] have repeated the various recommendations, with little change in practice in the intervening years.

Three years later, a paper published in Norway established that autistic people die on average 16 years before their peers across all medical categories and conditions.[17] While some learning-disabled and/or autistic people may have health issues that contribute to premature death, most do not. Learning disability and autism are not medical conditions. These stark mortality rates are a social rather than biological issue; people are dying early because they are not receiving appropriate health and social care and are not supported to lead flourishing lives.

So where is autism in this history?

This question leads to me touching on a key quandary in writing this book. Where does autism sit? Should I refer to 'learning-disabled and/or autistic people' throughout? Is that a cumbersome and problematic approach? What are we actually talking about here? In the end, I decided to run with the cumbersome while differentiating between specific aspects as and where appropriate, history being one of them.

Autism was 'discovered' or identified as a medical condition at different points across the 20th century. Leo Kanner, a child psychiatrist at John Hopkins University in Baltimore, is commonly held to have 'identified' autism. I put this in quotation marks because, while autism is a 'modern' condition, diagnostic categories are changeable and shaped by medical, social, political, economic and other contexts.

Question marks are also raised about the primacy of Kanner's discovery and the coincidence that Hans Asperger, paediatrician and Nazi supporter,[18] was coming to similar conclusions in a clinic in Austria around the same time. Silberman's meticulous research for *Neurotribes* uncovered how staff from the Austrian clinic ended up working with Kanner in the period leading up to his breakthrough, while Kanner himself remained oddly silent about Asperger's work across his career.

Kanner's famous paper 'Autistic disturbances of affective contact' was published in *The Nervous Child* in 1943[19] and a year later he published the term 'early infantile autism'.[20] In the original paper, Kanner presented a thoughtful description of the three girls and eight boys without much interpretation or judgement. He seems to have saved this for the high-achieving parents of the children whom he blamed for freezing out their children in their affections. Bruno Bettelheim, an Austrian academic of dubious background,[21] ran with this blame, with a focus on mothers, in the now discredited discussions about 'refrigerator mothers'.[22] It is important to note that this tendency to blame mothers continues to the present day despite it having no basis other than Kanner's fanciful and non-evidence-based thoughts.

In the UK, psychiatrist Lorna Wing is credited with introducing the term 'Asperger's syndrome' in her 1981 paper 'Asperger's syndrome: A clinical account', based on the work of

Asperger in the mid-20th century.[23] The 'triad of impairments'
– social communication, social interaction and imagination
– emerged around this time, and these have remained the key
characteristics of what has been called autism, autism spectrum
disorder/condition, Asperger syndrome and autism spectrum
conditions, despite being as flaky as the fridge-cold-mother stuff.

In the last two decades, the autistic community in the UK
and wider has become an established and increasingly influential
force. Neurodiversity is used to capture the strength and
diversity of ways of being, thinking and doing. Damian Milton
(@milton_damian), an autistic scholar-activist, has been a leading
proponent in both challenging conventional interpretations of
autism and working to generate change through initiatives such
as the Westminster Commission on Autism.* Introducing the
concept of the 'double empathy problem',[24] he argues that both
autistic and non-autistic people may find understanding and
communicating with each other tricky. Current articulations lay
the 'fault', the 'limitations', 'the problem' at the feet of a certain
set of people, effectively erasing the riches and value that autistic
people offer society. A serious and damaging oversight.

In 2009, the Autism Act was passed as an outcome of the *I
Exist* campaign by the National Autistic Society. This put a duty
on the government to produce an Autism Strategy and statutory
guidance for local authorities and the NHS to implement this
strategy. *Fulfilling and Rewarding Lives*[25] was published in 2011
and reviewed three years later with *Think Autism*.[26] This, let's
call it, pedestrian guidance talks the talk around training,
personalization, diagnosis, transition and the like.

In 2016, the punchier Westminster Commission published
a report *A Spectrum of Obstacles*.[27] The Commission involved
autistic people, academics and other experts, which more than
likely explains why the summary and report are crystal clear
and drenched in sensible recommendations. These include
better awareness of autistic people by health professionals, more

---

*   https://westminsterautismcommission.wordpress.com

training and resources to help autistic people understand what may happen in hospital, and the appointment of an Autism Director by NHS England.

Needless to say, implementing these recommendations proceeds at a snail's pace.

The Winterbourne View moment

As I touched upon in the Preface, a defining moment historically during this century was the screening of the *Panorama* investigation into the abuse of patients at Winterbourne View, a Bristol assessment and treatment unit (ATU) run by a company called Castlebeck, in 2011.

Patients were housed on the third floor of the building located on a business park on the edge of the town. This location, reminiscent of the removal of disabled people from towns and cities, sends chills through me. The story behind the programme packs a powerful and nasty punch as two members of the *Panorama* team moved to Bristol to capture the abuse after a staff member, Terry Bryan, made three separate complaints to Castlebeck and the Care Quality Commission. He then turned to the BBC. Terry Bryan, Mr Pantilledes... These kick-ass and largely unknown figures in a history too often kicked into the long grass.

In Bristol, 40 years after the Ely Hospital scandal, one journalist stayed in the rented accommodation to process the footage, while a second, Joe Casey, went to work as a support worker for five weeks. That it only took such a short space of time to capture enough undercover footage is one of the grimly appalling threads of this horror. Existing staff were apparently oblivious to new staff members coming in and witnessing the brutality being wreaked on patients, suggesting this was viewed as acceptable behaviour.

On the day the programme was aired, Casey reflected on the experience:

Simone was the recipient of the worst of the abuse that I witnessed, including being doused in water while fully clothed and later being taken outside on a cold March day where she lay shivering on the ground. It was a day that ended with the water from the vase of flowers that her parents had given her on a visit being poured over her head as she screamed on her bedroom floor. She was then taken into the bathroom for a second shower fully clothed and had mouthwash poured over her. It left me with my most haunting memory from my time undercover. At the end of that horrific day of abuse I was the only one in the group of support workers[*] who was not taking part.[†]

The *Panorama* programme was the making of a scandal and seemed to galvanize action among public, political and third-sector bodies. A concordat was signed by more than 40 organizations including the then Department of Health, Mencap, various royal and other colleges, the Council for Disabled Children and many more. The subsequent Winterbourne Joint Improvement Programme similarly had comprehensive sign-up and there was much talk (so much talk) of change, with an emphasis on getting people out of assessment and treatment units and back into their communities. Progress has been chillingly slow or even stagnant as *Transforming Care*[28] (the latest iteration in this grim unfolding) passed its March 2019 deadline having barely dented the numbers incarcerated. As I write this, Sky News have been meticulously trying to get to the bottom of the deaths of people in ATUs. The response to this by the Department of Health and Social Care pretty much repeats statements from 2011.[29]

What price human rights?

There has been a sizeable chunk of anti-discriminatory legislation in the last few decades including, in the UK, the Disability Discrimination Acts of 1995 and 2005 (now replaced

---

[*]   Six staff members received prison sentences and five received suspended sentences. Hill, A. (2012) 'Winterbourne View care home staff jailed for abusing residents.' *The Guardian*, 26 October. Accessed on 10/2/2020 at www.theguardian.com/society/2012/oct/26/ winterbourne-view-care-staff-jailed

[†]   http://news.bbc.co.uk/panorama/hi/front_page/newsid_9501000/9501531.stm

by the Equality Act 2010). Internationally, the United Nations Declaration on the Rights of Mentally Retarded Persons (1971) states that learning-disabled people have the same rights as everyone else. (Well, apart from the rights to marry and have children.) The Declaration on the Rights of Disabled People (1975) placed people in the position of 'citizens', emphasizing the rights of disabled people to enjoy as decent (and normal) a life as possible, and the UN Convention on the Rights of Persons with Disabilities was passed in 2006. Luke Clements, Professor of Law at the University of Leeds and Janet Read, Honorary Professor of Law and Politics at Cardiff University, highlight how, '[a]t its most basic', a human rights approach 'affirms without qualification that disabled people are not "other": they are unquestionably included within the category and meaning of what it is to be human, and may, therefore, expect all the rights derived from that status'.[30]

Again, we are back here to inclusion-phobia territory and othering. People are people. We are all human. These developments have not led to meaningful change in the lives of disabled people.

The problem remains that rights statements require action by governments, and this action, if there is any, is not always effective. It is also obvious and understandable that families are not typically well versed in the law, and taking legal action doesn't feature very high, if at all, on the list of tasks to get through, not least because of the large sums of money needed to do so.

A report by the Equality and Human Rights Committee to the UN in 2018[31] showed that half of the disabled people in the UK feel excluded and one in five experienced violations of their rights. In early 2020 steps towards legal action were taken with a pre-action legal letter issued to the Health and Social Care Secretary.[32]

Overlaying the historical with the personal

In 1982, our family decanted from Southend, Essex, to Henley-on-Thames, Oxfordshire, a few miles from Borocourt Hospital. A big old move generated by our mum's cracking promotion to building society manager. Our dad, a draftsman at Ford, transferred from Dagenham to Slough. My older sister, Tracey, was at university, and Sam was in her O level year (GCSEs were yet to break on to the scene). I moved to the local sixth form college to do A levels. After years of British seaside living, small-town life with pubs and clubs you could pretty much walk to was a revelation. My new life involved hanging out in pubs dotted about in Henley and surrounding villages, 'lock-ins' and someone always ready to drive home. Borocourt Hospital was a thing, a place of note. It was talked about without much mention beyond its existence. Imposing 19th-century buildings we would sometimes drive past.

I watched *Silent Minority* on YouTube after Connor died.

Silent minority.

In one scene the camera focuses in on a large wooden red engine sitting in the yard with wheels removed. Nigel Evans explains it was made by a group of boys from the local Borstal (young offenders institution) and donated to the hospital. Patients pushed it to the fence and tried to escape, which is why the wheels were removed.

Connor's paternal grandparents worked at the Borstal. His granny was a seamstress and granddad a guard. This link and my memories of passing the hospital on long, hot summer evenings filled me with a sadness I still can't quite make sense of. I didn't watch *Silent Minority* when it was aired. I was probably having too much of a good time.

A further connection with our experience and the documentary involved the response of Borocourt Hospital before the documentary was aired. A letter was sent to all staff members forbidding them to talk to the media. Thirty-two years later, Southern Health NHS Foundation Trust issued a similar warning to staff, this time electronically, as media pressure increased around Connor's death.

By the late 1990s we were beetling along in the disabled family side-track to life, which took in a cracking view of the mainstream while we remained firmly aware of our marginalized place outside it. Luckily, and partly as a result of health professionals proactively making connections between parents, we began to meet other families locally and friendships began to grow.

In 2003 a group of Oxfordshire families (and children) went to the House of Commons to the launch of the Mencap campaign about respite care for families, Breaking Point.[33] An unexpectedly memorable and fun day, given the focus. A mate's son, Matt, spontaneously breaking into a rendition of 'Happy Birthday' on local BBC News hearing it was MP Boris Johnson's birthday. Connor telling the taxi driver about London-based terrorist activity. A train journey home, laughing and loving with a carrier bag of differently sized M&S bevvies.

A few days later, an email exchange with the person I chatted to while the media stuff was unfolding downstairs revealed he was David Towell, author of *An Ordinary Life*. I remember feeling in awe of this coincidence, even while chuckling about it. Halfway through my PhD, I remained confident our children would lead ordinary lives. A disconnect and unknowing arrogance. We were pioneering a way forward with breath-taking naivety, oblivious to the families who came before us.

Our lives continued to play out against this historical backdrop as ten years later the CIPOLD report was published, two weeks before Connor was admitted to the unit. I remember feeling horror, shock and revulsion reading this, but did not for one moment link the findings to our family. Again, a heady mix of confidence and naivety. What was 'happening' didn't apply to our children. Our family.

A week or so after Connor died, the government response to the CIPOLD recommendations was published, including the refusal to set up a Mortality Review Board because it was too expensive.

This mix of the professional or 'official' with the devastatingly personal meant harrowing questions were raised in our minds about Connor's death and the apparently seamless attribution of natural causes to it by the NHS Trust responsible. Given the CIPOLD findings, we became concerned that this was typical practice. Via Twitter, we arranged a meeting with the then CEO of NHS England, David Nicholson, in March 2014. Rich and I turned up to the meeting having produced the Connor Manifesto the night before.* Rich pointed out we needed to have a plan for the meeting rather than rehash the details of Connor's obscene and preventable death. The meeting was efficiently brief, and Nicholson was surprisingly receptive to our requests. He agreed to commission a review into the deaths of all learning-disabled and/or autistic patients in Southern Health NHS Foundation Trust between 2011 and 2015, and followed through with this despite retiring a day or so later.

An international consultancy firm Mazars undertook the review, and the horror-filled findings included the identification of 337 premature deaths of learning-disabled patients in the care of the Trust, of which only two (Connor and another young man called Edward Hartley who died about six months after Connor†) were investigated. The average age of death was 56, lower than the findings of the CIPOLD review. This report reinforced how we are not much further on in many respects from the eugenic thinking of the last century.

The Mazars review was undertaken in the build-up to Connor's inquest and, again, became more salient as that process slowly and painfully unfolded. I think it was the Thursday of week 1 of his inquest that we found out that a patient called Henry had died in the same bath in the unit as Connor about six years earlier. Paul Bowen, QC, told us in the family room that morning. There was a delay in the start to the day as the coroner tried to work out how best to deal with this news. It is important to remember by this stage, over two years after Connor's death, that there had been a constant back and forth between Charlotte Haworth Hird, our solicitor, and the Trust about disclosing records and relevant documents. The Trust replied defensively at times, insisting everything had been disclosed.

Henry, who was 57, was undergoing a course of involuntary

---

* https://mydaftlife.com/2014/03/17/what-does-justiceforlb-look-like
† Edward's parents are still fighting for answers and accountability for his death.

electroconvulsive therapy (ECT) treatment when he had a seizure in the bath at the unit. There was no post-mortem or inquest, even though he had died in the care of the state. The coroner seemed concerned when this was presented to him and said that he would investigate further what had happened. I don't think I need to describe how devastating, shocking and bewildering this revelation was in an already harrowing space. A few weeks later, we received copies of police witness statements about Henry's death from the student nurse who was with Henry, the unit manager and the consultant who signed Henry's death certificate. The latter two staff members were present when Connor died. The statements contradicted each other: the student nurse said the manager was first to arrive in the bathroom and told him to leave; the manager said he didn't get to the bathroom until after the paramedics were on the scene.

On the basis of these new statements, the coroner concluded he was satisfied that Henry died of natural causes. When I raised the inconsistencies in the stories, he said that contradictions were inevitable after so much time.

Another life, another death, written off as natural.

Tues

Hi, is it Pink Day tomorrow? Thanks, Sara

Weds

Pink Day is Thursday. Connor is extremely excited about going to London for his birthday. We have been looking at how Hindus celebrate for Diwali. Connor said he is a Pagan and Pagans worship Stonehenge, Vince Noir and public transport!!

Perhaps Connor can tell you a little about Diwali. Pink tomorrow!!! Letter enclosed. Homework enc: counting in 5's. Have a great half term!

Chapter 3

The Early Days of Difference

BABIES, TODDLERS AND
DEVELOPMENTAL 'MILLSTONES'

Whoah. You have a baby.

A beautiful, truly wondrous baby. It may be your first baby, your only baby or one of a troupe of babies. A baby with the delicious freshly born smell, soft, warm skin that makes your heart melt and a love that makes you want to swaddle, cuddle and never let go.

At some point over the next few hours, weeks, months or years, you (or someone else) may start to recognize there is something unusual about your baby. You may compare her to her older brother or sister, niece or nephew, other babies at toddler groups. You may be shocked when a health visitor starts drawing crosses in your red baby development book. Or it may be you know about a particular condition before your baby is born, through prenatal testing or family history. However it happens, diagnosis (or the suggestion of something unnamed and unknown about yet) can be devastating and worrying. It can also be pretty much incidental or a relief offering explanation or understanding.

Learning-disabled and/or autistic children are often born into families with little or no experience of disability – a key issue which is often overlooked. Referring back to Erving Goffman's ideas explored in Chapter 1, 'the own' (people with learning disabilities or autism) and 'the wise' (those with deep insights into their lives) continue to be a select group in the UK. If you are not disabled yourself, do not have a disabled family member, and do not work in health, education or social care, the chances are that you may not come into contact with many disabled people. A strong mark of inclusion phobia.

In life, a 'diagnosis' is a word that is not usually associated with good things. It commonly signifies something is wrong – that you have an illness or a condition. Indeed, the word 'diagnosis' means to distinguish or discern a disease through symptoms – something that needs curing, medicating or treating.

But our children are often not sick or ill. Some will have other medical conditions; many will not. And yet it is to healthcare that we turn for answers.

There are myriad routes to a diagnosis of learning disability and/or autism, and these do not always happen in childhood. Diagnosis, usually a parent-dominated thing in the early days, can later become the choice or prerogative of the young person or adult. Some parents will deliberately not seek a diagnosis for their child, or may seek a diagnosis when they feel it is appropriate or necessary for different reasons. I know several parents with 'deliberately undiagnosed' children.* A sentence that, as I type it, underlines the social construction of what we are focusing on here. There are no clear boundaries to carve off sets of people who are identified as learning disabled and/or autistic – the conditions are culturally produced.

Evidence suggests that family experiences of childhood diagnosis have remained constant across the last two decades,[1] and I will draw on extracts from the Healthtalk project interviews here to illustrate different aspects of this process.

---

* A colleague left leaflets about Asperger syndrome lying around her home when her son was thinking of applying to university. She was concerned that he might be disadvantaged by the application process but was still not convinced he needed to seek diagnosis. He didn't bite, went on to do his degree and is now working in a job he dreamed of and living with his partner.

Developmental millstones[AQ]

Missing developmental milestones were a consistent feature among parents. Some children leapfrogged from milestone to milestone with little or no apparent groundwork, while others missed out stages such as crawling. Helen was a full-time carer and Jason a garage mechanic when I met them. Their son, Josh, was diagnosed with Asperger syndrome the previous year when he was five years old. Helen described how:

> And when he did speak it was sentences. Not like a normal child, where you get the words, the bus, the car, the whatever. Josh would sit there and he did full sentences. And we didn't do potty training. One minute he was in nappies and the next minute he was using the toilet of his own vocation. He had worked out how to stand up and use the toilet.

Sandy was a full-time carer to her two sons, both diagnosed with autism: Joseph when he was aged 23 months and Adam at 18 months. She described similar experiences to Helen:

> He didn't walk, this is Joseph the older one, he didn't walk until he was 15 months old, which I was a bit sort of concerned at, but then people say to you boys can be lazier than girls and he is a first child, he has got nobody to copy, but then the first time he did walk, he just sort of took off and shot across room and I just thought wow again [laughs]. So I don't know if he had been practising in secret something just as if to just suddenly go, and say, 'Hey look at me, I am off.'

If you step outside what can be experienced as punitive developmental milestones, these actions are quite extraordinary. Talking in sentences from the off, confident walking from nowhere and jumping to toilet-trained from nappies. Yet these achievements are downgraded to problematic or even pathological. Reframed as a sign that something is wrong. We come back to inclusion phobia here as mechanisms for identifying difference, and diagnosis work to differentiate and exclude.

Other parents also described their children's unusual

speech patterns. Children talked late or made sounds unlike conventional baby 'babble'. Some children repeated phrases they heard from the television or other family members. Amanda, a yoga instructor, and her husband, a catering manager, have two autistic children. When I interviewed Amanda, Louis was five and Georgia three. Louis was diagnosed aged three after he stopped talking six months earlier. His sister was referred to the child development centre when she was two years old. Amanda's son was a big Disney fan and could recite chunks from films perfectly. She joked that his first sentence was the *Toy Story* phrase 'From infinity to beyond'.

Connor was an unusually 'good' baby. A baby who did not demand attention, content to watch life unfold from a play mat or pushchair. A baby who demonstrated a quiet curiosity with life around him without the need for interaction or apparent thirst or hunger. Sandy described Joseph as the perfect baby who was never any bother and Caron's son, Leo, was a 'good baby':

> He didn't smile at people, you know, other children were beginning to babble and say words. He didn't say anything at all really. He just seemed to be very much in his own world. That sounds such a cliché but we could just put him in his bouncer and he would happily sit there all day and not murmur and he didn't get hungry or get thirsty, you know, even as he got older he would never ask for things, we would have to tell him, you know do you want something to eat, do you want something to drink. He would never ask for anything. I mean I knew straight away I could just tell.

In contrast, another mother described how her son 'came out screaming and that was all he did; scream and scream and scream. He would feed for a couple of minutes, go to sleep and then wake up and scream for two or three hours.'

There are layers of recognizing unusualness among parents and different levels of certainty about this. Daniel was a full-time carer to Jonathon, 13, who was diagnosed with autism when he was four years old:

Okay. It all began of course when Jonathon was born and right from the very first moment we noticed there was something unusual about our child, from the very day he was born. Not that there was anything wrong, but he seemed special. And obviously right from the very first moment everybody told us that all parents think their children are special, but we knew there was something different. He had a different kind of awareness about him.

This intuition is something many parents experience. A kind of 'I knew, I just didn't know what I knew'. The things parents notice often do not sit within developmental milestones. Why would they? Milestones are a medicalized and measurable checklist, whereas parents notice more ethereal points: a baby who looks bored, an unusual worldliness. Christine was a full-time carer to her daughter Elisabeth, 13, who was diagnosed with autism and learning disabilities. Christine described how:

> You know, she had this look even from when she was a tiny baby. I got the impression that she thought you were really stupid. It was the look she gave you as if to say you are just so pathetic. Do you know it is awful strange, even from when she was about six or seven months, like she had this play mat and it had animal noises on and like she didn't like you holding her hand or she didn't like you picking her up or anything and I would have her hand and I would push it onto this sheep sound and it would be 'baaa' like that and she would look as if to say, 'Now isn't that stupid. Why on earth are you doing that?'

Some parents have vague feelings about difference and remain ambivalent about going to the GP because it can be tricky to articulate this sense. Rachel, a full-time carer to two autistic boys aged nine and six, said although she had niggles, she didn't want to go to her GP and say 'I've got a naughty boy'. Appearing to be bored or baffled by conventional baby activities and play are not easy to discuss with health professionals. I remember a frustrating and isolating conversation walking through the woods in early spring with another young mother when I tried to put my unease about something I couldn't quite pin down into words. She brushed it aside with a few words of dismissal.

Some parents notice nothing and find out almost accidentally that their child is autistic. Vikki, a teacher, and Nick, a design engineer, had two sons, aged ten and eight. Their younger son, Peter, was diagnosed with Asperger syndrome aged five. Vikki described how they were surprised by a nursery school teacher raising concerns about their son at a parents' evening. They identified their son's actions as strengths:

> Well I think initially we thought we had a gifted child because he started preschool and I can remember, there I was. I had a son at nursery, and my youngest was starting a preschool at two and a half and they were lining up the plastic animals and they were saying moo cows, baa sheep, whatever and he looked, 'That is a hippopotamus.' And I was thinking, oh yes, wonderfully gifted child and we thought nothing more of it. So he went through the preschool and then got accepted in the same nursery as my older son and for a year we thought well nothing untoward has been said. He is obviously working hard and he wasn't forthcoming about what he had done, but the nursery staff didn't tell us what he hadn't done.

I asked the couple if they were surprised when Peter was diagnosed within six months of that meeting. Nick replied:

> Not really having thought about it, because from the...it is like being on top a diving board, isn't it? You kind of think you have got this gifted and talented child. I think it was further for us to fall into the water from that position of thinking, you know, we had such a talented wonderfully eloquent child into this diagnosis but when we kind of sat back and observed what he was like in comparison to his peers there was – you couldn't question that there was something different about him.

In a similar situation, Dot, a full-time carer to Joe, was approached by a student teacher when her son was seven years old:

It was a teacher in school that was a student teacher. She said to me, 'I think you should maybe take him to the doctors.' And I thought he had hurt himself or something in the playground and then I said, 'What has he done?' She said, 'He is having difficulty concentrating.' I said, 'Well he always has difficulty concentrating unless it is Batman' or whatever his little obsession was at the time and she said, 'Well you know, it is not up to me to say and I am leaving' – because it was by the end of term and she was only a student – but she said, 'Have you ever thought he might be autistic?' And I was like…I didn't know what to say to her.

A slow burn

A study by Laura Crane and colleagues in 2016 surveyed 1047 parents in the UK to explore their experiences of getting a diagnosis for their children.[2] They identified a 3.5-year delay between raising concerns with health professionals and getting a diagnosis of autism for their children, with an initial one-year delay in contacting professionals. Ninety-six per cent of parents said they noticed their children's difference, and the authors present a deficit-drenched and medicalized list of these differences: impairments in socialization; the presence of behavioural rigidity and/or the displaying of behavioural problems; milestone delays; failure to develop normal [sic] pretend play; rituals/obsessions. This shoehorning of quiet curiosity, an ability to intensely focus on things and not engaging in pretend play is the beginning of a lifetime of respite instead of holidays, learning outcomes instead of fun and a placement rather than a home.

The road to diagnosis can be intensely stressful and emotional for parents, in part due to the length of time it can take, and there are considerable implications around parents not feeling supported.[3] Parents can be fobbed off with comments about boys developing later than girls or more broadly dismissed. This can generate obvious frustration. Carolanne, a teacher, saw 23 professionals before her daughter was finally diagnosed with Asperger syndrome aged 14. Caron's son was not diagnosed until he was three years old, despite her certainty from the age of six months. She thinks, in part, that health professionals did not take her seriously because she was a very young mother, but she had grown up in a family with a lot of young cousins so had considerable experience around babies. Christine also felt very let down by professionals who she thinks looked down on her because she is working class. These dismissals can be wounding for parents, lead to further delay in diagnoses and potentially harm relationships with health professionals.

I wrote about the dismissal of parental concerns by GPs[4] and presented an early draft of this at a GP conference in Oxford. Naively facing an unexpectedly frosty audience, I was told I had no idea how many worried parents GPs saw in their surgeries. One woman caught up with me in the corridor afterwards as I scuttled off and said I really ought to check the medical records of these children because the parents' accounts were clearly exaggerated. It was insightful that parents were continuing to experience dismissal of their concerns even by proxy.

I sensibly gained a GP co-author at that point and we came up with the idea that GPs could say to parents that while she or he was not concerned, as the parent was, the parent could keep a diary for two weeks, jotting down examples of things that concerned them, and bring this back to the surgery for further discussion. Our rationale was the 'worried well' parents may peel away when diary entries turn out to be thin, while parents of yet to be diagnosed children could return with the list generating a more substantial base for the GP to work through with them.

The delay in diagnosis is important because it means that children are left with parents who possibly do not understand them. It must be overwhelming to be constantly misunderstood, particularly by those you are closest to. Parents can be left with frustration and puzzlement, feeling they do not understand their children and are somehow failing.

The route to diagnosis varies considerably too once a child has been referred. Katrina was a full-time carer to her daughter, then 11, and son aged eight. Callum was diagnosed with autism after a three-week residential assessment during which he was observed 24 hours a day, was filmed and had therapy sessions. I cannot even begin to imagine what this experience is like to endure. Katrina's account of this process captures the complicated, emotional and practically exhausting process it can be:

> I think really horrible in one way, really horrible, you know, just being away from home I didn't like and being away from my daughter and knowing that she needed me too. But I knew that it was like the last stop. I knew that at the end of that they would either give me a diagnosis or they would send me away and say it is just a development thing, or it is emotional behavioural problems and I was a bad parent, that is kind of like what I expected. I dreaded that being said. I dreaded it all being put back on me. I knew that wasn't right because I am just so attentive with both my children and my daughter is so the other end of the scale, you know, she excels at everything and is a bit of a natural but I like to think I have played a part too and I just feel why hasn't it worked like that for Callum? So I knew it wasn't me but you do kind of like have to go through everything before it is eliminated that it is not a parent, you know it is not a parenting problem, it is a condition. So yes, that gave me a sense of relief as well.

During this process, parents are often caught in a 'liminal' space* – of 'knowing and not knowing', dreading and hoping. Amanda described her fear before her son's diagnosis and how she dipped in and out of the internet, which was not helpful:

> But I must say now that the fear I felt beforehand it is not, nothing as bad as you fear, is it? You know it is not that bad. He will go to school. He will do things. You know, it's...you have got to try and stay positive really as much as you can, and, you know, hope for the best. But yes, we started going on the internet but

---

* Liminality, an anthropological concept, means being in between different statuses like child and adult. Families, or often parents, can occupy a liminal space between being a family and becoming a family with a disabled child.

you just get absolutely reams and reams of things. It is too much. I think we looked for a while and then I stopped because I was just... I don't know, I was just making myself quite anxious about the whole thing so I just sort of, I will wait until, you know, the diagnosis and then take it from there.

Sandy had pretty much decided Joseph was autistic and felt prepared to receive the diagnosis:

And then I started looking into it after I spoke to this other mum and I picked a leaflet up from the library and I think there are about eight different sort of criteria, sort of traits of autism that are listed and then realized that Joseph had about seven of them. And I thought well he must be. So in a way when we actually got the diagnosis through from the paediatrician we kind of prepared ourselves for it anyway. We were quite expecting it I think and from then on that meant that we knew what we were dealing with.

Being told

- How do you tell parents or a parent that their child is learning disabled and/or autistic?

- What words do you use and how do you frame the diagnosis?

- How do you manage the appointment: the timing, the length of time, the setting?

There has been a shift since medics encouraged parents to leave their children in hospital and forget about them in the 1950s, 1960s and 1970s, but I am not sure how far we have moved from delivering a diagnosis couched in such negativity that it leaves the child with no imagined future. Crane's study found 66% of parents were satisfied with how the consultant conducted themselves. Less than two thirds.

Anyone seen that low bar? Good practice included: handling the diagnosis in a thoughtful and sensitive manner; clearly explaining the diagnosis to the parent; consulting with the parent as co-experts; demonstrating a high degree of knowledge and empathy. Not identified by these authors, though of key importance, is allowing the child to be a child still. A beautiful, little human with their whole lives ahead of them.

There were examples of being told the news in a sensitive, thoughtful way, and this could be recalled years later. Helen, for example, described how:

> She was excellent. I mean if I could describe her, she is professional from the top of her head to the tips of her toes and we had obviously got to know her and we formed a relationship with her from the outset. She is just that sort of person. She has got such good interpersonal skills and she puts you at ease and I kept very detailed behaviour sheets for her and she saw Joseph a few times and she didn't – I think it was the way she approached it – she knew she had got to break it to us gently but she didn't hold back and I think that was the best way to do it. And she offered a couple of leaflets to start with. She said I don't want to bombard you because you need to go away and take this in.

Picking out what it was about the delivery of the diagnosis that was important to Helen, the relationship she and her partner had with this psychologist is key. Her interpersonal skills, clear explanation and rationale and understanding that she should not 'bombard' the parents with information, are sensitive and thoughtful. Parents are often going to be devastated hearing this news, and Helen said she could not take much in beyond learning that her son was autistic at that point.

Responses to the diagnosis or diagnoses comprise a right old smorgasbord of reactions including relief, shock, distress, despair, vindication and equanimity. Bobbi was a retired make-up artist working as a part-time administrator, and her husband ran his own business. Their younger son, Charlie, was diagnosed with autism when he was five years old. Bobbi had been pushing for answers for three years. She described experiencing intense frustration at how much work it took to get her son diagnosed and the moment she was told as 'utter relief':

> So I think that when I realized that early on Charlie was unbelievably brilliant at numbers, really good at numbers, and had a real affection for languages that were 'sing songy'. Things like that then, I don't know, just something snapped and I just thought 'yes maybe' and googled it and brought up a load of stuff. And I think it was through the National Autistic Society first that I learnt mainly about it. And a lot of things made a lot of sense, a lot of sense. And then to get the diagnosis for that one day with all the doctors there, it was like ping, ping, ping, like light bulb moments going off all over the place and it was a real relief to be honest with you, it really was, because for me as a mum it made me feel like I did understand my son. Because for a lot of years I didn't feel like I did, you know, maybe not years, but for a good space of time, I really didn't think I understood him at all.

It is so important to frame the diagnosis in a way that doesn't close down the child's future. Bobbi treats it as a starting point for the family rather than the end of the world and recognizes her son's strengths as strengths. Charlie is 'unbelievably brilliant at numbers'. Dot similarly read up about autism after the intervention by the student teacher and described being delighted when her son was diagnosed when he was seven:

> I went to see the doctor. She had an assistant with her so I could talk to her and she would be working with Joe at the side and they were trying to get him to do some art work but within that whole assessment which was just over an hour, I think, an hour and a half. She said, 'Oh he is clearly Asperger's.' And I just wanted to jump up and kiss her because I thought, 'Thank God for that.' I know... I thought it was Asperger's after doing all the reading and thought, 'Oh at last.'

And so that is what I did. But I was really, really happy. I rang everybody as soon as I got home.

I felt like I had to prove that I wasn't going mad, you know, people think that you are just making excuses. People think that you are not disciplinarian enough but one of the things that I really was glad about, I mean people have different views about smacking children and disciplining children and things, and I always really didn't ever want to smack, but there were times when Joe was just like lying on the floor in the supermarket, because he wouldn't come in, he didn't like the lights, he didn't like, there was lots of things, the noise, you just feel like smacking his legs or something but I didn't obviously but I thought after that diagnosis thank goodness I didn't do anything like that because the guilt of having punished him for doing something that he can't help, I would have felt absolutely awful.

I mean I felt bad enough as it was because I didn't know how to handle him, but then I thought well how would I know how to handle him? Babies aren't born with instruction books. You don't know how to look after them and I didn't know anyone who had a child with Asperger's. So you know as well as for Joe because I thought this is good now. He will get help. I also thought, 'Now people will take me seriously. I can explain to them what Asperger's is. I can explain to Joe what Asperger's is. We can move forward now. I can't wait to get my hand on all them services.' [laughs] So I really celebrated that night.

Like Bobbi, Dot views this as a beginning for Joe. She also captures the complexity of the experience for parents, of trying to reconcile actions and behaviours with expectations and confusion about how to bring up a child like her son who did not sit within the guidance laid out in child-rearing manuals. I remember having a wry chuckle with Dot when she said she could not wait to get her hands on 'all them services'. Our naivety as parents, thinking that support is there when you finally get the magic key to open that door. The expectation that a whole raft of specialist professionals are there, ready to ease your child into the world with this new understanding.

One of the things I learned after Connor died, and with the remarkable support that #JusticeforLB generated from members of the public with little or no experience of disability, was that people assume families get the support they need from health, social care and education professionals. Until you actually enter this world, you have no idea how patchy it is. The Crane study found that 40% of parents received no post-diagnostic support and less than 25% were provided with a direct offer of help.[5]

Getting the diagnosis can generate a maelstrom of emotions and feelings. Some parents liken it to a form of bereavement. Tony captures how he felt when his son was diagnosed:

> Oh. It is not, when you get the diagnosis it is not such a shock, because you know that there is something wrong in a big way. You know what your son is like. You wouldn't have been there if you didn't know what he was like. In fact since his birth we have spent arguing with people there is something different about our son so to be told there is something different on the one hand it is actually a relief you know at last somebody has said, 'Yes you have not been making this up just because you are proud. There is something different about your son.' So it was a great relief.
>
> But on the other hand it also comes as a shock, a complete shock. It is like you have gone from fighting to get people to believe to suddenly having to face up to the reality. And I think it is like a bereavement, it is just like a bereavement. It hurts. You know I think I was crying every day, whenever I was in my car, never in front of people, I was on my own surrounded by metal. I just cracked up every day for must have been near, or nearly a year and I still break down in tears every now and then if I stop to think about the reality of my son's life and what may or may not lie ahead for him.

Tony relates his tears and anguish in part to his fears for his son's life and future in a world that is not always hospitable to people who are different. This is where professionals can make a substantial difference by presenting the diagnosis with sensitivity and care while making it clear that the child's life is not over, that they are not consigned to some sort of barren hinterland.

The diagnostic process can be 'smoother' and swifter when it involves a second child or subsequent children in a family.[6] This can generate different layers of upset. Rachel described it as 'really sad', while Sandy said:

> That was a very big blow for us personally as a family because I think really we just thought we had a normal little boy and then all of a sudden he is autistic as well. And the first thing that hits you is, is there something wrong with me? Can I have a normal child? The boys are still very, very different. It took me a good 18 months I think. I almost went through a grieving because the little boy that I should have had felt as though he had been taken away and that was very hard to deal with actually. I did go through quite a down stage and I suppose even then we were just looking into autism. How it would affect the boys, trying to understand what was going through their heads. And sometimes you think you understand something and then they do something that you are totally not expecting which is, which is normal now I suppose [laughs].

Sandy's account incorporates a growing sense of developing a space for what is 'normal for us' which is what happens. Once the ship of 'normal' has sailed, families tend to knuckle down, have a bit of a shufti about and start to redefine normality. This can work well, particularly when layers around the family embrace this, too. Again, professionals can support this by being open and flexible.

Information

How much information parents would like to be given at that key appointment will vary from family to family. The Crane study found that information tailored to the family is important. Caron, below, describes how she would have liked more information on the day and how she felt the door was being closed on her, whereas Helen earlier said she was not able to take much in beyond the actual diagnosis:

> I would have liked the hospital when they gave the diagnosis to give more information yes. Obviously I have been forced to get my own. But a lot of people that I have met who have children with autism, it has all been the same for them as well, they have all said, 'Right your child is autistic, see ya.' And then that is it, then you are just left to deal with... I mean for a lot of people they are not going to be aware that their child has it, so when they do find out I am sure it can come as a blow and then to just be told to go home and cope with it, you know it is stressful, you know, because autism isn't something that they are going to grow out of, they are going to be like it forever and nowhere, you know, the doctors don't seem to take that on board, how the parent could be feeling. You know, it seems to just always be about the child and of course, you know, the child is important but the parent is as well, because they are the one that has got to look after the child.

The child is typically the focus, and parents can feel invisible as humans in these encounters and in the communications between appointments, despite the burden of engaging with and negotiating the sometimes thorny terrain of services and support falling on parents. Asking parents 'And how are you?' is such a small thing to do and yet can make people feel less alone.

Connor's diagnosis

Because Connor's diagnosis happened during the earliest days of the internet, I relied on baby manuals at first. It was heart-wrenching to look up concerns in these books and be sent to a list of 'for further information' addresses in the back of the book rather than any engagement within the text. Another graphic example of exclusion as our beautiful baby boy was booted straight out of the manual that had served his older sister so well. His diagnosis came about via the missed milestone route a few months after I'd asked our GP to refer him to a paediatrician at the local hospital. I was worried that he wasn't talking and barely walking at around 18 months old. As I mentioned earlier, he was also an incredibly good baby, while also, apparently randomly, descending into inconsolable screaming periods.

After asking a few questions and looking at Connor who was cheerfully playing with his toy bus, the paediatrician said he was just a boy and sent us away. A journey home feeling slightly sheepish about being a time-wasting, overly protective parent, combined with a hefty dose of relief. A few weeks later, during his 18-month developmental check, Connor 'failed' each task, ceremoniously gaining a cross in each box in the red book where just a few pages earlier was written 'a perfectly normal baby', and I was faced with a clearly concerned health visitor.

About six months later, with significant intervention from me, newly armed with the early version of Dr Google, Netscape Navigator, Connor was diagnosed with mental retardation/ learning disabilities and a chromosome disorder called Klinefelter syndrome. Connor's version of Klinefelter syndrome was apparently a mosaic form, which, we were told, meant he may have milder effects of the condition (or not). Autism was added to his collection of diagnoses a year or so later. I was given the original news over the telephone by the GP who used a 'there's good news and bad news' technique which I wouldn't recommend. The 'good news' was that it wasn't Fragile X syndrome a different genetic condition, which was my thinking at that time. It was Klinefelter syndrome. It was a few days before Christmas.

Looking back now, I wince at the uselessness of much of the information that is passed to families. It is so important to think about *how* parents are told about this stuff and *what* they are told. It may be a passing conversation for a consultant in a day full of appointments, children and families, but these words stay with us, I suspect, forever. The mosaic part of Connor's diagnosis was never explained in a meaningful way. I would later chuck it into the odd consultation with a geneticist or other relevant consultant hoping to be enlightened, and never was.

The most important aspect to being told that your child or children are learning disabled and/or autistic is captured by Catherine who had two teenage daughters diagnosed with autism:

> We had some fortunate interactions with medical professionals around the time each girl was diagnosed. We were put into contact with a number of sensitive, honest, and very helpful doctors who understood that we wanted an answer and provided it. What I didn't want at that time, and still don't want, is somebody telling me what my child's future is going to be. I will be eternally grateful to one senior, very experienced neurologist, who wrote in his report something to the effect of yes, my child had very severe developmental delays but he couldn't predict the future; sometimes these children could surprise you. That one small comment made a big difference to me.

I'll end this chapter with a story about a young man we recently met.

Rich's new colleague, her partner and his 13-year-old son, Max, came round for the first time a few months ago for some nosh. Rosie and her partner, Jack, were also home that weekend. Max was a bit overwhelmed by the change in plan not to cycle to ours because of heavy rain and disappeared into the back room to listen to the US jazz music he loves from a small section of inter-war years. He later rejoined us.

As he'd not eaten much, I asked if he wanted a frankfurter. Oh, yes. He loved frankfurters. Rich got the packet out of the fridge. Max's eyes lit up. The best kind, apparently. I warmed it up in a pan of water and handed it to him on the only clean plate we had left. A small, shiny, metal, slightly high-rimmed plate.

He looked at it for a moment. And then said slowly with a deep and rich conviction, 'That. Is. So. Sad.' He took his phone out of his pocket and photographed the offending 'furter' to put it on

Instagram. 'Did you actually boil it?' he asked me with wide-eyed incredulity.

The next few hours were filled with laughter, hilarity, warmth and humanity. A few weeks later, Rich got an email from Max's dad saying how much he'd enjoyed the evening. Max still shows people the photo of the frankfurter.

I tell this story here to contrast the divide or even chasm between professional speak about learning disability, autism and difference and the richness that diversity within and beyond families generates. Being told that we would probably need respite from our son when he reached his teens was not only a brutal statement in that moment, but also (temporarily) erased the joy, love, brilliance, knowledge, generosity and thoughtfulness that Connor would contribute to our family. It framed him firmly as a problem to be managed and, by extension, us as a problem family. Our evening with Max was fun and memorable. We all had a bloody good time. Please don't ignore the love, the joy and the fun families and friends have.

Chapter 4

Childhood Challenges and Wondrousness

Families with learning-disabled and/or autistic children typically involve additional layers of wondrousness, labour, challenge – and sometimes despair.

These challenges are often – not always, but often – an outcome of the lack of 'fit' between the child, on one hand, and, on the other, an outcome of the lack of 'fit' between the child, on one hand, and strong expectations that children will act and behave in narrowly defined ways. These expectations also shape the organization and delivery of services, support, education, social care and wider society.

There is an enduring tendency to use a deficit model of childhood disability lens which obscures much of what we should *value*.

Back in 1997, in response to attempts to use models of grief to frame parents' experiences of diagnosis, online instructor at DeVrys University, Dona Avery wrote:

> I have seen a 5th stage, and it is not Acceptance or Hope of a Cure. It is learning that an unborn perfect child was one conceived by society, not me, and that the actual child I was gifted with is perfectly fine.[1]

It is also the case that the work involved in parenting disabled children – what Eva Kittay, an American philosopher, calls 'dependency work'[2] – can be intense and often unrecognized and unsupported.

A chapter on childhood could fill a book, so here I narrow the focus to some of the key challenges that come up again and again: parental and professional knowledge, sibling experiences, going out in public, meetings, managing expectations and advice giving.

First, some facts and research evidence.

What do we know?

Around 32% of disabled children are brought up in single-parent households (compared with 22% of non-disabled children).[3] It is not clear if the numbers of single-parent families with learning-disabled children relate to differences in social class.[4]

What is important and undisputed is that single-parent households face increased levels of poverty which can be compounded by the additional labour associated with having disabled children. We also know that around half of disabled children live with a disabled parent and around 25% have disabled siblings.[5] Grim and seemingly entrenched evidence points to a link between social class, economic disadvantage, disability and debt. I don't want to get into the finer detail of this here, other than to flag up that disability can both be costly and reduce the capacity of parents to undertake paid employment (the latter is a cost that still falls disproportionately on women, a subject I return to in the next chapter):

> On almost every measure of material deprivation, disabled children are more likely than other children to live in households which are unable to afford things that are generally regarded as important and ordinary for children in the twenty-first century, such as having more than one pair of shoes, access to outside play space, participating in a leisure activity once a month or buying some basic toys.[6]

So with this less than cheery context, let's move on to a consideration of parental expertise.

Developing expertise

Parents are typically experts in their children's lives, whether or not their children are disabled. We know our children, love and largely understand them, get their idiosyncrasies, likes, dislikes, interests and know what makes them happy, although this knowledge can wax and wane over time. For many parents, the goal is (or possibly should be) to make sure their children, whatever age, are happy, fulfilled, content, loved and safe. To help equip them to flourish in their adult lives.

In the early days, weeks, months of their child acquiring a label, some parents will try to find out every bit of information they can from the relevant health (or social care) professionals, other parents, the internet, books, television and any other media. Parents will often fly with this detail and, through the process of wanting to know more in order to better care for their children, may develop an expertise in whatever diagnosis their children have. Those parents whose children are disabled without a label can struggle here as they are working without known parameters. The organization SWAN ('syndromes without a name') was set up to support families in this situation.*

Parents absorb this information, weaving it in and around the edges of the baby, infant, toddler, child or even adult they love with such intensity. In some ways, it forms part of the parenting care package. It is useful but it does not define their child or children within the context of family, love and everyday life. It is a piece of family life which is typically a jumble of different pieces with varying shapes, flavours and colours. Sometimes this one piece will shine brightly or be more absorbing or frustrating, and this will again be part of shifting family dynamics.

---

* See www.undiagnosed.org.uk/support_information/what-does-swan-or-being-undiagnosed-mean

Weaving professional and personal knowledge

Kittay wrote about the peculiar overlap between the different knowledges parents and professionals have:

> There are, on the one hand, the imposing (often impressive and sometimes worthless) professional knowledges that are being applied to your child. On the other hand, there is one's deep and intimate knowledge of this child, a knowledge that is, however, curtailed by one's limitations in training and expertise.[7]

Trying to negotiate these professional and personal knowledges can be tricky, yet working together is essential to generate the necessary conditions to support children to lead their best lives. Health and social care professionals, no matter how brilliant, engaged, focused, determined and informed, may sometimes through necessity given the demands of the job, form disembodied, often medicalized and atomized positions around the particular label or condition, in a process that can leave the child an object rather than a little human. This can be all too painfully obvious to parents.

Complicating things further and more broadly is the balance professionals need to strike between recognizing the expertise of parents while also providing appropriate support for them. I've lost count of the times I and other parents said that 'we don't know what we don't know' as we discovered something completely new but important enough that we can only think health or social care professionals assumed we knew about it. Bewildered conversations around 'Do you get respite?' 'Eh?' 'Have you heard about ESA?' 'No, what is it?'

A recent serious case review[8] recorded how a mother was asked if she had had a carer's assessment before her daughter died. 'I don't know,' she replied, 'though a social worker did ask me how I felt once.'

One thing that has puzzled me over the years (and clearly continues, as shown in conversations with other parents either in person or via social media) is the way in which professionals sometimes ignore parental expertise rather than seizing upon it as a means of helping the child most effectively and making their own job slightly easier. Not listening to parents can generate risks to the children or young people (as evidenced in numerous inquests, including Connor's, which have been live-tweeted in recent years*). There is ample evidence of the consistent advocacy role that parents play on behalf of their learning-disabled and/or autistic children, and yet we are often ignored or sidelined.

Perhaps part of the puzzle is that parents are intensely concerned about their children's wellbeing and may inadvertently antagonize professionals, or not interact or engage with the professional with an expected level of deference. A clash of knowledges. Jacquie, who had five autistic children, said:

> But in general a lot of the time I find that professionals don't want parents to tell them things. You have to feed their egos and there has got to be a particular way that you can feed things into conversations so that they think they have come up with the answers. A bit like dealing with men really [laughs]. And if you have done that then sometimes it is easier, but really you should be able to speak straight because these are important issues. You can't afford to wait to six months if your child is being bullied and if you get one appointment every six months or you are waiting here.

Running alongside this sometimes contested expertise can be what Chris Goodey has described as 'insane' behaviour by professionals. (This is one of those – I'm sure many – points in this book in which sucking up indignation, frustration or umbrage over such a statement is necessary. Please hang in here: this is an important and fascinating point!) Goodey uses the example of parents of a six-year-old learning-disabled girl trying to get her a place in a local primary school. The head teacher uses a set of disconnected reasons why the school is not an appropriate setting for the child which include not being able to sit quietly in assembly.

---

*   George Julian, an independent consultant, has live-tweeted several inquests which can be found on Twitter. Have a look, for example, at @TozerInquest, @JusticeforLB and @ JoeInquest.

'How many six-year-old children can sit quietly in assembly?' her parents ask.

The head moves around a series of shifting positions – very much like playing one of those very early computer games that involved moving a rectangle to hit a ball at different targets – to persist in her core argument that this school is not appropriate for their child. This example reminds me of my short-lived attempt to get Connor a place in the primary school literally across the road from us, where his older sister Rosie was thriving. The head teacher's protestations basically consisted of 'He can't because...' with no clue as to the substance of what the 'because' consisted of. Pondering out loud about this on Twitter recently, another mother replied saying:

> Sounds identical to the conversation we had... school where I had been a member of staff before it split into infant and junior so new infant head. We got an answer eventually – it's epilepsy – 'tuts' – PE – wall bars...

Goodey's point is that the actions of these professionals and the anxiety they are demonstrating is disproportionate to the potential threat posed. The scrabbling to shut down any whiff of certain children attending a school is extreme. Another mother joined in the Twitter discussion with an alternative, refreshing experience:

> We were so very fortunate the head at our village primary said 'What can I do to help E be happy here?' Apart from one teacher who didn't want anything to do with learning disability (presumably in case it was catching) the school were amazing for the 5.5 yrs she was there.

Goodey's use of 'insane' may seem extreme, but there is a thread of 'insanity' that runs through the childhood (well, life, really) of disabled children. A consistent series of blocks, obstructions, flaky excuses and an almost myopic focus on deficit which erases the good stuff. Too often, we do not notice this insanity. It is normalized practice and, given that it takes time for parents to become 'wise', can take some time to recognize.

Moral pioneering

There is no rulebook about how to bring up a learning-disabled and/or autistic child. As I mentioned earlier, when Connor was a pup, the internet was a relatively new beast, and social media, as we now know it, did not exist. There were clunky forums and comment sections under online articles, but little of the current, ferociously burgeoning, space offered by social media platforms like Twitter, Instagram or WhatsApp. We take the information we find or are given, sort through it, weigh it up, take advice where we can and make parenting decisions.

Pressing decisions are to do with how far parents are prepared to go in order to help or encourage their children to fit in. Rayna Rapp, an American anthropologist, calls parents 'moral pioneers' in making these decisions.[9] This suggests that parents are on their own in this activity. Parents decide what is most important in their children's lives (or potential futures), and this may involve taking 'calculated risks'.[10] We may expect and demand too much from our children as we try to carve out space for an imagined future for them, placing what may be damaging and unattainable burdens on their cheeky little shoulders.

The use of the intervention Applied Behavioural Analysis (ABA) is an obvious example here. This approach involves breaking down the components of an action, such as saying a particular word or clapping, into small steps and using a reward (and punishment in some versions) system to repeatedly encourage the child to achieve the task. This is a controversial approach[11] and I feel sad and ashamed to have put Connor through a light version of this for many months when he was around three years old. The myth of a window of opportunity in which it is possible to whizz your child back on to a mainstream track can be compelling.

Useable information that meets all parents' needs

We know finding *useable* information is a problem for families,[12] particularly about issues such as access and entitlements to services and benefits, and how to find key contacts.

Unsurprisingly, families want clear, jargon-free information in different formats, with a mix of short and more in-depth guides for particular key periods.[13]

There are specific considerations when working with or supporting families at the intersection of marginalized identities, such as ethnic minority groups, transgender and sexuality, age and disability. For example, we know that particular difficulties can be experienced by families from South Asian communities.[14]

There is little research that focuses on the disabled child's perspective, and the voices of black and Asian children in disability research have been almost silent despite their experiences being uniquely different to those of white children[15] – for example, experiencing individual and institutional racism as well as disablism. Intersectional analyses reveal multiple forms of oppression that serve to further marginalize and disempower people. There is a strong argument that we need to prioritize a social justice framework in tackling systemic rigidities.[16] That is, we need to focus on rooting out inequalities and unfairness.

Nura Aabe, the mother of an autistic young man, set up a group for migrant communities in Bristol called Autism Independence and, in collaboration with colleagues from Bristol University, has conducted research about the importance of cultural views of autism.[17] One participant in their qualitative study said:

> People in Somalia have not heard of autism before. No, they haven't. There is no autistic person in Somalia. There isn't anybody who doesn't talk in Somalia. I haven't seen anybody. And people said they haven't seen anyone who don't talk and have something like autism in Somalia.[18]

The lack of recognition of autism, together with cultural attitudes that stigmatize mental illness, led parents to experience social isolation and attempts to hide their children rather than seeking support. Furthermore, parents were encouraged to believe that their child would recover (or they should take them back to Somalia) which could interfere with or disrupt decision making about how best to support their children. Adding to these difficulties were challenges parents faced in trying to understand and navigate unfamiliar health and social care systems, findings replicated in other research. One study of six African immigrant mothers, Munroe's study of six African mothers recommends that clinicians (and social care professionals) should initiate open conversations about parents' experience and wellbeing, allowing space to discuss 'difficult emotions and internal conflicts'.[19]

Useable information is a surprisingly tricky beast to crack. Important pieces of information are often acquired via other parents in groups like Nura's. I remember finding out about Education and Support Allowance one Friday night when having a few bevvies with mates who had children at Connor's school. I had no idea Connor had been entitled to this allowance for a good year at that point. Gail Hanrahan, now CEO of a local support charity, Oxfordshire Family Support Network (OxFSN), told me that same evening through gritted teeth that information about this allowance was clearly detailed in the transition guide OxFSN had produced for local families. A guide I had proofread several months earlier.

The sharing of meaningful information involves more than handing over a leaflet. Accessible and culturally appropriate information is essential. As is recognizing that passing on a snippet at one point in time does not mean that information has been understood or absorbed. Family life is busy, messy and distracting. I can only begin to imagine parents saying 'Blimey, I just got told about ESA again by the social worker...'

Siblings
A brief foray into research focusing on siblings of learning-disabled and/or autistic children was not a comfortable activity.

Much falls into the toe-curling and jaw-clenching space of psychological functioning and negative framing. Just two examples on the first page of the search: 'The impact of autism on siblings'[20] and 'The psychophysiological impact of ASD on siblings'.[21] This is reminiscent of the parenting literature from a couple of decades ago before corrective work kicked in, rejecting the outright pathological and losing the largely trumped-up bleak. Given the importance attached to evidence-based practice, this sibling literature is depressing as it must generate or reinforce negative attitudes and misunderstandings. It is so important to wear a clear and critical lens when looking at the evidence base around learning disability and autism.

Sisters and brothers are intricate and integral bods in family life, sometimes acting as informal little supporters within the family structure.[22] I feel uncomfortable about identifying siblings as 'young carers' and was relieved to see a recent study[23] highlighting this point. The authors argue that current focuses on a binary of 'positive' and 'negative' outcomes in terms of siblings' wellbeing hinder our understanding of the experiences of families, and that we need an 'alternative experience-sensitive informed framework from where autism research and interventions can be led in partnership with all family members'.[24]

The experience-sensitive approach taken is grounded in family life rather than 'scientific' concepts; and the unfolding understanding generated is apparent in the findings which stand out as a pocket of brilliance in this too often bleak research landscape. An example of the framing of the findings:

> Seven sisters share a room with their autistic sibling, so after school hours they spend the majority of their time at home around their autistic sibling. Most of the data provided evidence that the sisters attuned themselves greatly to their sibling by knowing the things that the sibling enjoyed, as well as the skills and positive attributes of the sibling. All the sisters provided extensive details about their siblings' interests and joys such as their favourite games, music, activities, food, and colours. Some

sisters state that they like to teach their siblings new leisure skills, such as painting or cycling.[25]

The extracts of data are reminiscent of the ways in which our children, and other siblings we know, talk:

> My sister has a talent for completing beautiful colour patterns. She loves detail and she will never give up till all coloured boxes or tiles look the same. She has an elegant taste in music and she absolutely concentrates on the sound of the bass or drums. She has a great memory and although she can't read she knows how to find her favourite CDs or videos. I am not sure if that is autism or it's her. I would like to think it's just my sister. I don't live with autism. I live with my sister.[26]

The overall findings include frustrations and struggles in a humanizing way rather than erasing love. This, for example, is not present in much of the research – joys and unique moments of warmth alongside the difficult stuff.

The authors found that participants were resourceful, empathetic, tolerant and loving. Rather than raising caution about the impact of caring responsibilities on siblings, doing tasks typically viewed as non-normative by some researchers (and by implication potentially harmful to the wellbeing of siblings) is normal to the siblings and is framed as 'helping out'. This underlines how 'problems' are generated by dominant assumptions which do not take into account people's skills and abilities or how they understand and interpret their lives. The siblings felt it was important to carve out private time and wanted access to ordinary activities. They also wished their parents did not try to 'fix things' as they all wanted acceptance of the autistic identity of their siblings. This is a fascinating insight, as we saw earlier how parents are moral pioneers in trying to carve space for their children which can involve attempts to make them fit in better.

Other corrective research describes 'chaotic childhoods' with a 'normal for us' framing:[27]

I mean it's just who you are. It's normality, isn't it, for an autistic sibling? That's your normality, and I would have thought it very strange to have siblings who aren't autistic.

Chaotic is not necessarily a negative term, and the ups and downs, bumps and brilliance of lives in families with disabled children can be fine. It is the lack of appropriate support and the impact of that gap on family members that needs attention.

In the Healthtalk project, interviews with siblings captured a rich range of experiences and reflections. Eloise, for example, was 18 when her younger brother, aged 12, was diagnosed with Asperger syndrome the year before her interview. She presented a picture of frustrations and irritations reminiscent of many older siblings, with additional bits of puzzlement:

It was, it was a mixture. I mean obviously every big sister finds their little brother annoying, but there were times when I just didn't understand why he wouldn't put the yellow t-shirt on... You were trying to get him to just do something and he wouldn't do it, and he didn't know what and he was getting very upset over something that was very tiny... There didn't seem to be any explanation about why he would get so upset when the Hoover was turned on or why there were certain smells that he just, or why he would suddenly appear very rude or...which again caused problems at school.

This extract echoes the frustrations we heard from parents in the previous chapter. Without the diagnosis to shed light on why her brother might be sensitive to particular noises or smells, for example, Eloise is left confused and frustrated. This puzzlement is an odd one. Once there is an explanation – an answer to why children find supermarkets distressing, for example – the irritation and frustration disappears. Sensory overload makes sense and accommodations kick in. It is as if we have one lens to look at children's actions, and once we are able to slightly tilt this lens, a new picture becomes clear. One that makes a lot more sense to us and one that is fine. The problem then is that other people outside of 'the own' and 'the wise' continue to use the original lens. This can generate problems that are difficult to resolve.

Later in the interview, Eloise was asked whether or not she told friends that her brother was autistic if they were coming round to her house:

> No. I mean, now chances are he'll be sitting reading or on the computer or doing something. He won't really, he might say hello, but he won't... I mean my best friend knows that he has, he's on the autistic spectrum, but that's just through conversation and also through knowing him for quite a few years now, rather than just coming round a few times or something. But in terms of someone new coming round I don't really, I don't say anything. It's not obvious. And it's not...there's nothing that they couldn't do around him that they would do to someone they hadn't met before or...I just...it wouldn't, yeah [laughs].

We didn't tell children who visited our house that Connor was autistic or learning disabled. One of Tom's close friends said that he did not realize Connor was autistic until after he died. Tom himself found out when he was at a friend's house watching TV and the friend's dad referred to it. I remember him coming home and mentioning it. Within families, once over the initial bump of finding out a child is disabled, we just are. It is often simply not relevant. Kids muck in together and get on with it. Parents parent. The work gets done. Inclusion phobia does not begin in childhood, and families should really be used as an exemplar of how society could be.

I think sibling relationships can offer a reciprocated generosity of being that is deeply powerful and too often ignored. While parents try, as we saw above, to 'fix things' to try to generate a space for children, siblings can be more accepting. Membership of 'the wise' can be a more organic happening for siblings, developing in real time rather than in a catch-up-while-firefighting scenario.

Ellie, 17, had a younger brother aged 13 who was diagnosed with autism when he was two. She described how she wished he could have been 'normal' and different to how he was. She also ends her account here with a clear and definite statement of her love for him:

> I guess there's always been times where I've, it sounds horrible but I have hated him. Not because he's autistic, but because he wasn't normal. I have rarely ever thought that, but it was when there was a lot of people in our house. I just regretted that he was like it. Then I've got more used to it, and just more accepting that he's not going to change very much, but the more he learns, the more he's going to be able to do different things, and the more he enjoys, like he never used to be able to go to the cinema, because he used to get scared of the dark. Now he absolutely loves it, and it's really nice just to take him to that. But there's times when he has got really angry, and he has lashed out, bitten me before, and I had to go hospital because he broke my skin and there's like, there's lots of different things that have made me just want him to be a bit different, but I've never stopped ever like loving him as like my brother.

Going out in public

Going out in public with children who may act unusually can be quite an experience, and was the focus of my PhD research back in the day. It brings in a lot of sociological aspects around rule breaking and disruption, making visible the strength of the often-unspoken rules that guide or govern us in public. You only have to walk along the street with a child shouting or making unusual gestures to find strangers commenting or glaring at you, effectively calling you out for poor parenting. My first academic paper was called '"Busy behaviour" in the "land of the golden M"',[28] inspired by one mother's description of her daughter's enjoyment (or sometimes distress) of public places as 'busy behaviour' as she repeatedly pinged metal railings or lay on the floor and refused to move. Many parents describe McDonalds, or the 'land of the golden M', as a favoured destination because the food is served quickly, it is always the same and there is a lot of bustle, which means families don't stand out.

'Rule breaking' in public can be wondrous. There's a park across the road from us, and over the years a mother and young son would walk around it. He would dance in wide and elaborate patterns alongside her in a way that was mesmerizing. He embraced and used the space with an absorbing and quiet sense of joy. And in the process he created something beautiful, transforming the space and demonstrating other imaginings.

Reflections, concerns, humour and anxiety about going out in public were recounted in the Healthtalk project, and I've heard and shared countless anecdotes of public encounters. It can be distressing to experience strangers making judgements about your family. Ellie, for example, recalls:

> We were in a shop once and there was an elderly couple. They don't know everything about it, but someone said that he just seemed like he had half a brain. And it was quite insulting because he was only about six and I was about ten and you just you don't say that about people anyway, but then the person behind the shop like told them he's autistic, and I don't even know him. And it was nice to know that some people do know. But I don't really know what people think of him, but he used to like fall on the floor and start kicking off and people just walk over him. And I guess that was why I didn't really want to go out, because I just didn't want to see people's reactions. So I think people kind of think he's really different and like odd, and they don't really think that it's disability. They just think he's like either playing up or being strange I guess.

And how do you feel about all of that?

Oh well, that's why I was rather protective. It really upsets me, and it gets me angry that anyone would say that about anyone really. I don't think it's right just to say anything about anyone like that. But I suppose it's harder with autistic children because they don't look any different. They look normal, then they can be walking along and all of sudden twirl around like a princess. It's, if he's a boy at like five foot something, it's kind of strange. It's funny to me, because I know that he's doing it because he's being him. But no one else will know and they might think he's a bit strange but I guess that's what I was worried about. But then I learnt that if people are going to see him like that then they're not really worth thinking about at all.

I suspect parents talk a lot about their experiences of being in public because public censure can be wounding. Jane described feeling mortified and embarrassed when her son, who was three when she was interviewed, has a tantrum, typically in the doctors' surgery. These experiences can be funny when recalling them, but they are distressing in the moment and are often an outcome of something unavoidable or unexpected as we work hard to reduce disruption. Another mother Nicki said:

> I mean sometimes you are really close to tears and you just want to get up and walk out, but he is not going to learn anything by that so we just have to sort of hang on in there. And one time he was crying, I had to pick my Mum and Dad up from the airport and the flight was delayed and he cried for three hours in the airport and I didn't have a buggy with me. I usually have, we usually have a disabled buggy for him. And he was kicking, and he was screaming and he was pulling hair, and I just had to hold on to him and just wait because that is all I could do. It is funny looking back on it, but it isn't so funny at the time [laughs]. And a couple of weeks later we were in B&Q or, you know, a DIY shop and Tyler was playing with some things in the shop and it was time to go and he didn't want to go. So you know he screamed a bit and banged his chest a bit and he was stood near a little boy who was also playing with the same things and the little boy's mother came over and took his hand and moved him away from Tyler because she didn't want him being near Tyler and I said, 'It is not contagious you know.' But it hurt, it really hurt that somebody felt they should remove their child from where my child was.

I'm not sure health or social care professionals can fully understand the gauntlet families run, sometimes on a daily basis, either negotiating unforgiving and unenlightened members of the public, picking our way to any number of appointments, making phone calls, completing forms, as well as dealing with individual family members who need attention at that particular moment. It is also the case that parents can harden to the public scrutiny and feel more confident about fronting it, which can be, in itself, liberating, as Sandra describes:

> I suppose I used to be quite embarrassed that people were looking at me and I used to think when Joseph was having a paddy in a shop or something I used to think, oh God, people are going to think he is horrible and he is not and I used to be saying all the time, 'Oh I am sorry, my little boy is autistic, and he can't help it' and feel like I needed to explain to people what was going on. And that actually carried on for a couple of years and then one day I realized I had actually got round Sainsbury's and I hadn't done it. I hadn't apologised for my boys being autistic and I actually said to my husband when we came out, 'Do you realize we have just gone all the way round. We have done a big shop with both the boys and we haven't apologised to anybody once for the way they are' [...] But I quite enjoy talking about the boys and why they are the way they are now. I am not fazed. I am proud of them. I'm very proud of them. But it did take quite a while for this feeling of having to apologise. And I thought why should I? They are just my boys. So I don't know. I suddenly smelt the coffee or something. I don't know.

This realization, this acceptance, this developing knowledge, the shifting from being an outsider to one of 'the wise', has a peculiarity about it. It takes time and involves having to question and reflect on so much that we typically take for granted. However, alongside this developing knowledge is a reinforced understanding that our children do not fit in wider society and are not really welcome. This is where the potential for health and social care professionals to play a powerful role in creating space in which children do fit kicks in, and yet is little considered in practice. Treating the whole family as fully human and valued members of society should take little time and minimal effort and yet can be immensely important to families.

This was clearly reflected in the sparkling tweet contributions. For example:

> I also remember exactly where I was when Ed psych said I was being reasonable. I think psychologists call these flashbulb memories – like remembering where you were when Diana died – shows how significant these micro kindnesses are. (Katherine Runswick-Cole – @K_Runswick_Cole)

> Principal of my son's primary school, whenever there was a tough meeting re his behaviour, always started by asking everyone to take a min to remind ourselves how much progress he had made. Always ensured a v positive meeting. (Ann Brehony – @ AnnBrehony)

> Remember in the very early days post diagnosis a speech and language therapist referring to our son as a 'dear little boy'. As indeed he was but we found it very touching at the time. (Jane #stopbrexit – @everhopeful1000)

> The Speech Language Therapist who began her letter describing my son's assessment findings with a few sentences explaining what a pleasure Adam had been to spend time with, and what a happy soul he was. It meant a lot to me. (Mark Wilberforce – @M_Wilberforce)

Meetings, appointments and communication

I was struck quite soon after Connor died about the number of meetings I attended over the years, many of which amounted to little more than box ticking. So many meeting permutations with social workers, paediatricians, psychiatrists, psychologists, a dietician, an endocrinologist, another psychiatrist. Repeating the same dismal deficit-laden narrative to a new face with the expectation of something happening when too often it didn't.

I wrote an account of one meeting which took place at Slade House years before Connor died in the unit on that site:

'A picture of Mum?'
Posted on 4 June 2011

One thing that doesn't happen so much now that Laughing Boy is 16, is endless (often meaningless) appointments with professionals. Countless hours have been spent travelling, waiting and meeting a range of different people in different settings. One series of appointments, four years ago, was with a psychologist geezer (Psych Sid*) about LB's 'challenging' behaviour. These appointments seemed particularly pointless as Psych didn't want LB present.

One appointment day, LB had an inset day so I thought great! Good opportunity for Psych and LB to meet. I told LB where we were going, and to give him credit, he went upstairs and put on his ELC police tabard (age 2), his baseball cap and his orange binoculars. Dressed to impress, we set off to the clinic.

Psych Sid was surprised by LB's presence and told him to do some drawing at a small table. There followed an awkward 30 mins where Psych asked me questions and I'd say 'Well, why don't you ask him?' Nah. As the appointment drew to a painful close, Psych asked LB to show him what he had drawn. LB came over with a piece of paper covered in neat brown lines. 'Ah, lovely,' said Psych Sid. 'Is that a picture of Mum?' 'No,' said LB, 'it's a lot of brown lines.'

I remember walking back to the car from that meeting, knowing we would never get that time back, not realizing the car was parked within view of the unit Connor would later die in. So much bureaucracy and paperwork with so little meaningful action in practice. It is as if there is a 'diagnosis = a heap of meetings across years' formula. An addiction to meetings which takes little or no account of the work (practical and emotional) involved for families: dread; advance preparation; negotiating family and/or work commitments; travel and time; sometimes tears and upset.

Parents in the Healthtalk project were clear about how intimidating meetings with professionals could be and the obfuscation that can happen. As an aside, one of the older carers I talked to, discussed further in Chapter 7, said the advice she would give to her younger self was 'be braver and speak out'. This is good advice, though easier said than done when you are sitting discussing your child with a set of strangers who may never have met her. Mike here focuses on the use of acronyms:

> So when I first went in you could be intimidated and a lot of parents are intimidated because the professionals talk in professional language, lots of acronyms. I always stop people. [...] I have learned that. If anybody uses an acronym I say, 'What does that mean?' Because I understand it is to speed up the conversation, you can talk in acronyms if you are all professional. But if there is a parent there who doesn't understand and is not used to all that kind of language, I say, 'Can you speak in simple English, words of one or two syllables?' Because you have got to because I think they try, I think at first some of them do try and they do overawe you, overpower you with all this language and so you end up going in. They talk about your son or daughter and you come out and you are just absolutely bemused. You don't know what has gone on, you know.

Acronyms and jargon are exclusionary and intimidating. Professionals typically hold the power in these meetings, and I would not have had the nerve in the early days to ask people to explain what they meant by certain terms or acronyms. I would have remained baffled. We know there are communication issues and a lack of accessible information for families with ethnic minority backgrounds. The use of acronyms and jargon magnifies this.

When Connor was approaching adulthood, I did question the social worker when she emailed to let me know we had been 'successful at panel' and had been given an 'indicative budget of £x'. I didn't understand what these statements meant. I later found out she recorded in the notes: 'Mum was very hostile and asked what a panel was.'

I'll deal with the first two issues here before moving on to a personal bugbear.

First, avoid acronyms and jargon.

Second, try to put yourself in the shoes of families, try to understand what they are experiencing.

Third, don't call me 'Mum'. This is demeaning, disrespectful and diminishing. The most generous interpretation I can come up with is lazy shorthand. Please use people's names, and if you do not know them, ask. Again, a tiny and very straightforward thing to change.

Caron felt very strongly that professionals had been judgemental about her and would not take her concerns about her son's development seriously. This continued in her relationship with health professionals at the time of the interview:

Generally how would you describe your dealings with professionals?

I think that if I was more like other business women, a sort of woman, instead of a stay-at-home mum I would have been dealt with a lot better. I do believe. I think if they knew what I was talking about and I went in there and I was right 'blah blah blah', they would be treating me a lot better than me going well I think there is something wrong with him 'blah blah blah'. Do you know what I mean? I think they do stereotype, yes, that is what I think. [...] Even now, you know, if I ever try and ring his paediatrician, well I have tried to three times in the last month and I haven't got a single reply, I can never speak to her and she will never ring back. So it is still not very good no.

'A deep breath and a little kindness'

Sparkling examples of tiny shifts in practice or thoughtful layers of icing were abundant in the tweets. Just a taster here:

Psychiatrist from specialist CAMHS service who sent photos pre home visit (and Secretary remembered daughter's love of pugs so included pug memes in letter). Despite being in suit, let dogs climb all over him and even sat next to snakes despite being wary all to build rapport. (Emma Dalrymple – @emmadimps)

And actually, credit needs to go to specialist CAMHS again – it was part of the Parent as Therapist model where we (husband & I) sat down with psychologist who does home visits and clinical psychologist who leads & supervises to discuss how to build relationship before even met E. (Emma Dalrymple – @emmadimps)

She chooses the amount of time they spend together (from a choice of three) and this is displayed on an app. They post her a letter every week before each session, addressed to her and written in a way that's accessible. This has formed a 'template' for any new professional. (Emma Dalrymple – @emmadimps)

My boy broke his arm this summer. Local hospital staff from reception to radiology treated him w kindness & respect, found out his special interests, took time w him, explained everything that would happen, distracted him from discomfort with comic book obscuria & excellent puns. Worlds away from the 'big' hospital where the staff are more expert but also too busy to take a breath and see that the child needs care, not just treatment. It's all it takes, a deep breath and a little kindness. (Emma Burns – @betaburns)

The cardiologist wrote a personal letter to J thanking him for being so good during the MRI afterwards. Outstanding work.

Made the difference between having a scan to check on aortic stem and not. Made the whole experience 'not that bad' for J. And that was the aim. (Louise – @mustntgrumble)

Being thoughtful could also involve being proactive in terms of supporting the family. Catherine Rule tweeted that the consultant who saw her daughter, about something unrelated to autism, noted the family were struggling after talking to them and made an urgent referral to CAMHS. Holistic care, as Catherine commented. Similarly:

The most amazing Orthoptist who can not only complete calm fun eye tests with both my children (no small miracle) but also asks about their general well-being and that of the family and makes referrals and supporting letters to other HCPs, social care, etc. Above and beyond! (Dr Lauran Doak – @LauranDoak)

Working effectively with families involves putting the child first, thinking about the whole family, being flexible, allowing parents to check documents and reports before they are circulated, checking assumptions, listening and being willing to run with 'unconventional ideas':

Neurologist who always began by asking us: 'where do you think we are up to' in long process to decide if W could have epilepsy surgery. He always checked so he never made assumptions about what we'd taken in, so no surprises. He gave us a sense of control in scary times. (Katherine Runswick-Cole – @K_Runswick_Cole)

The notion of control that Katherine mentions here is so important. There can be fearful decision making to be done around surgery, medication or other interventions, and feeling that you are being treated as an equal partner in these decisions is important.

Many of the tweets referred to shifts in practice in terms of the spaces of hospitals and GP surgeries, and the additional time professionals allowed in order to provide appropriate and supportive care. Some of the examples here touch upon the recommendations of the Westminster Commission for Autism report. Out-of-hours home visits, alternatives to the main waiting room, positioning on the consultation list, additional time, talking carefully through what was going to happen, all contributed to positive encounters. There were more specific examples, such as offering a home visit to reassure the child and a consultant sitting on the stairs to allow the child to remain in their bedroom, letting the child touch all the clocks in the surgery before seeing the GP, and making sure the reception radio is turned off before the child's appointment:

> Recovery ward making sure Ear Defenders were put on straight after op, machines silenced and lights down low, curtains shut and that I was there before 20 yo woke then put in a side ward. (Superstes – @freedom4lou)

> Never forget nurse who arranged for the big prince to have his own room for cardiology appts. He arrived to a drs room with his name on the door, access to a computer & WiFi. Drs came to his room not theirs! Anxiety plummeted!! (Marianne SB – @mariannesb37)

Again, these are tiny and effective adjustments. Generic good practice with additional layers of person-centred care woven throughout.

While more unusual now, seeing the same health or social care professional can lead to the development of trust and understanding. Leise Cooper (@leiselily) described how the special care dental service have seen her son since he was five years old and they built his trust in them at his pace: 'Forgot to say he's 20 now and has great teeth! Which he cleans himself! Things I thought would never happen.' Other families had similarly warm and positive stories:

> Son's social worker in children's. Years and years' worth of wonderfulness. Kept him at home for as long as possible by making services adapt then made sure provision was in same city

(spannered by corporate buying them out but she didn't know that would happen). (Dr Chris P – @CATS_Chris)

The support worker at my son's residential school, who has seen him through 3 years, and is now helping him get ready to move to residential college. She spent yesterday helping him declutter (MAMMOTH TASK!) ready for moving & then took him to see the Spiderman movie as a treat. (Anne Worrall-Davies – @a_wdavies)

Honesty and openness around what support or resources are available is always a good step. Often parents know and are told that resources are very scarce. If a parent is bold enough to counter this by saying that their child really needs x, y or z, they can be made to feel they will be depriving another child of that resource. This works as an effective silencing mechanism as it introduces a moral argument about equity while leaving families (a) wondering if they have somehow been greedy or selfish and (b) usually without the requested resource. A double whammy.

Moreover, as parents we often do not understand the legal rights, duties and obligations the state has towards our children, or how we can operationalize these rights to make sure our children receive appropriate support, particularly in a period of austerity. In talking with human rights specialists about various resource-related issues since Connor died, I have often been told, 'The family should judicially review that decision...' The problem is we don't know what this means in practice or how to do it (certainly without a handy wedge of cash to do so).

Again, it is back to parenting without a map and with some of the (few) signposts kicked over in the ditch or pointing the wrong way. This generates frustration, depression, fear, anxiety and exhaustion.

'Insane' advice

Alongside meetings and the managing of expectations is the giving of advice to families, which may either be deeply appreciated or generate despair. Featherstone quotes a professional who became a parent and said, 'Before I had Peter I gave out programs that would have taken all day. I don't know when I expected mothers to change diapers, sort laundry or buy groceries'.[29] Setting aside the wincing gendering here, it is not uncommon for parents to be advised to take actions that are simply 'insane' (to borrow again from Goodey).

Just one example, although I am sure parents will have their own examples of 'insane' advice tucked away in their back pockets. Alison and Tony here are talking about the advice they were given to try to get their son to sleep at night:

Tony: Work it out for ourselves. Yes. Exactly. You know but it was at the time when he wasn't sleeping and all the usual nuggets used to come out about how to get a child to sleep which none of them ever worked.

Alison: Oh yes. She used to tell us put him to bed and get a chair and sit in the bedroom with him until he went to sleep.

Tony: Yes. We did that and at 4 o'clock in the morning I was falling asleep on this chair and he was wide awake.

Alison: I said do you realize how long it takes to get this child to sleep and then eventually keep moving the chair further and further to the door?

Tony: Cracking idea that.

A final recap before we leave childhood for a consideration of love's labour:

- Try to understand that the child is part of a family, big or small. She is loved off the planet and, like her siblings, brings joy and immense pride to her parents and wider family.

- Try not to dent or damage that love and pride by a careless focus on process and bureaucracy. It only takes seconds to remain human and recognize the child as a child. We are forced to recount our children's deficits, what they can't do, over and over again. The grimness of this could be reduced by a social worker or paediatrician recognizing the child in front of them and commenting on him or her as a small person.

- Think about the layers of emotional, physical and practical work parents typically do around parenting, meetings, campaigning and fighting for scarce resources.

- Try to minimize your contribution to that by thinking about the timing, location and point of appointments, and being clear in terms of expectation management.

- Call parents by their names.

18.1.2011

Is there any chance Connor could have another watch? We have tried to explain that you do not need to throw a watch away if the strap is broken. ;-)

Chapter 5

Love's Labour and More

In structuring and writing this book, it became clear that a separate chapter was necessary to focus on the experiences of parents and, in particular, mothers. This is because of the enduring tendency for mothers to be the main caregivers, and because when a child or children are disabled, this mothering involves a deep intensity and complexity.

It is not always the mother, of course. Nicki and her partner Mark made the decision that Mark would work part-time to fit around holidays and after school, and men can obviously be single parents. Mark Neary* again comes to mind as a cracking example of a dad who ticks the advocate/activist box as well as fitting his paid work around his son's life for many years. However, it is typically women's work and we do women a disservice to pretend otherwise.

In her wonderful book *Love's Labour*,[1] Eva Kittay calls this 'dependency work' and is very clear that it is *work*. The three strands of maternal practice identified by American feminist philosopher Sarah Ruddick[2] – preservative love, fostering growth and training for social acceptance – become so dense when children are disabled that dependency work can grow exponentially. At the very heart of this work is the almost

---

* https://markneary1dotcom1.wordpress.com

impossible task of trying to redefine normalcy to include what is normal for our children while socializing the world as best we can so that it accepts our children. This dependency work, and the contribution it makes to society, is both extraordinary and typically ignored.

Back in the day, Katherine Runswick-Cole and I met at what was then the annual Disability Studies conference at Lancaster University. We felt uncomfortable and out of place in that space because we were not disabled ourselves but were mothers of disabled children. We wrote about this experience in a paper[3] which was initially brutally pilloried by one of the three peer reviewers but went on to be the top-cited paper in the journal the following year.* We highlighted the liminal space we then occupied within Disability Studies, and argued that mothers develop an unrecognized special competence and what is an undervalued role as activist mothers. Disability Studies as a field has changed since then. There is more engagement with non-disabled family members, but the points about not recognizing or valuing the work mothers do remain more enduring.

Employment and dependency work

We know that there is tension between paid employment and being the main caregiver in families with disabled children. An international systematic review which included the UK found that the structures that exclude autistic children have a knock-on effect on the employment opportunities for parents, in particular mothers.[4] Gnawing on my fist as I type, it is important once again to highlight that the child is not the problem here. The structures and system, and the people working within these, militate against genuinely flexible working. Informal childcare arrangements with family, friends and neighbours are often less forthcoming than they may be for other families, and there is often a lack

---

* We wrote a second paper on this topic in 2019 (see Chapter 8). Both peer reviewers asked us to remove mention of the earlier review in the text. We decided it was one of those 'pick your battles carefully' moments and removed the offending sentence.

of appropriate childcare cover after school and in the holidays. Little attention is paid to supporting women to return to paid employment.

Rachel gave up her job as a social worker because she knew helping her older son to settle in school would take considerable work. By the time her younger son was also diagnosed, she decided to continue to stay at home because he needed her to be calm both before and after school. In a similar way that dependency work is unrecognized, little apparent attention is paid to these sometimes dramatic career shifts (or withdrawal from the labour market) that some women experience. As Rachel said, 'Getting used to the idea of not working is a bit odd, I will be honest with you, because I always did. So being at home all day is very, very strange.'

Paid work is a key point at which the trajectories of parents of disabled children can take a substantially different path to those of non-disabled children. Having a child does not usually permanently derail careers in the 21st century. For mothers like Rachel and many others, being compelled to put their children ahead of their own desire to work is complicated. Giving up work can entail a loss of identity, a reduction in finances, a lessening of social contact and interaction – and we know how undervalued dependency work is. This can be a heady mix for mothers to deal with. It is a big step to decide not to work, or simply not be able to work, when you anticipated working alongside having children, and it has substantial short- and long-term impacts on later life. At the time of writing, Carer's Allowance is a paltry £66.15 a week, and dependency work and the accompanying skills count for very little in the field of paid employment.

For some parents, dependency work can develop into an unexpected job and career openings which can be fulfilling. From our jaunt to the House of Commons mentioned in Chapter 2, Gail Hanrahan, together with another mother, Jan Sunman, went on to set up a charity called Oxfordshire Family Support Group* which has been quietly effective and productive in helping local

---

* www.oxfsn.org.uk

families for the past decade. The strength of the organization has been the expertise and experience of those involved and it now employs a number of mothers as family advocates.

The tasks of dependency work

Kittay argues that dependency workers direct their energies and attention to their dependency work, which involves additional tasks over and above the typical parenting jobs such as feeding, dressing, carting around to school, the park, shops, bath and bedtime. It can also be more enduring. Some examples:

- administering medication and medical interventions
- personal hygiene tasks
- advocating and activism
- negotiating (and policing) support and services
- attending appointments
- writing letters or emails
- picking up incontinence products from soulless business parks
- changing nappies on a public toilet floor
- reading reports
- filling in forms
- additional washing.

Parents are constantly trying to prevent the downgrading of children to bundles of burden and toil rather than fully fledged little people.

It is everyday life as a parent with a ton of stuff on top. Furthermore, staying at home without a break can be exhausting. Many parents are able to release their children into a world of childcare opportunities around school, including childminders and after-school clubs and activities, and eventually children take themselves to and from school. The lack of opportunities for our children to do this, because of a lack of appropriate support, can lead to parents experiencing isolation and stress.

To do this dependency work, energy is key, and this can be disrupted by the boundless energy of children, their rule-breaking tendencies and the way in which sleep may not be high on their agenda. Jane recounts the challenges involved in constantly watching her son without a break:

> I find that anything that he needs in terms of like nappies because he is still incontinent or Disability Living Allowance, everything is a weight on your shoulder because the services are so short. We don't...we have only just started having respite care now and he is three and a half and it is a real sort of struggle. That has been a real challenge because we are with him 24 hours a day, 24/7, we care for him 24/7 and some days he will just not let up. From six o'clock he is up in the morning until seven o'clock at night, he is up and he is around the house, and he has no sense of danger, and a very, very low pain threshold. So at any minute he can do something and you have got to sort of stop him and tell him or he can have an accident and he won't tell you. So there is always something sort of in the day that will prove challenging with him.

Amanda, similarly, describes this exhaustion:

> And you know it is full on from...they get up in the morning and from them going to bed, when they are in obviously. I am quite relaxed now that they are both at school. It is full on. You know, until they are asleep you know and then it is usually sort of half nine, quarter to ten before we have tidied up and we sit down and [sigh] oh [laughs].

There is yet another tricky balancing act here for parents (and for me in writing this book): how to convey the challenges and sometimes the enormity of the work involved without reinforcing stereotypical understandings of disability as burdensome and overwhelmingly negative.

Heart-sink bureaucracy

High up on the list of the heart-sink moments of any parent of a disabled child is the filling in of forms relating to benefits and allowances, and the despair this task generates. The questions can be almost impossible to answer, and there is nowhere in this process to add in any reference to the child as a child as opposed to a diagnosis and set of deficits. It feels as though we are forced into a continuous cycle of proving our children are less than human while trying to chip through this deficit wall to share their brilliance, beauty and joy.

In March 2012 I wrote a blog post about my experience of filling in Connor's Education and Support Allowance form, and I share part of it here to provide an example of this. I was being kind of humorous in writing it, but the experience was bleak, worrying and time-consuming. I kept putting the form back in the large brown envelope to try to regain pieces of sanity around completing it:

> To start the claim, I did a phone interview with JobCentre Plus (JCP) which lasted about 40 minutes and included mind-boggling questions like 'Who is the head of your household?' The next step was to get a sick note (???) from the GP. He sensibly gave LB an indefinite sick note. This was returned by JCP as it needed to be backdated by three months. Back to the GP for second sick note. Indefinitely sick since November 2011.
>
> So a medical practitioner has authorized LB's removal from job seeking indefinitely. But that's no longer enough. There is a 'Limited capability to work' questionnaire to fill in, so that experts (undefined) from Atos* can judge whether or not LB has legitimate access to allowances in place of paid employment. Well. Where to start? It's 20 pages long, covering questions about medical condition, treatment/medication, physical and 'mental, cognitive and intellectual functions'.
>
> Questionnaires are always flawed but this one is legendary in its crapness. I feel strongly that if someone can't fill in the

---

* Atos is an information technology company.

questionnaire themselves, because they have severe learning disabilities, then it's a done deal. Bin the questionnaire, it's pretty obvious that this person is going to have a limited capability for work. I'm not suggesting at all that people with severe learning disabilities are not ever capable of paid employment, but that some limiting parameters are in place in terms of the engagement with the process. And if they can't engage with the process, some other poor bugger (often parent) will have to instead to fill it in on their behalf.

Compounding this, the content of the questionnaire is baffling and ultimately meaningless. For example, it asked if you could do a 'simple task like setting an alarm clock'? How is setting an alarm clock a simple task? You've got to be able to tell the time for starters before you even turn to the clock. Just a small consideration I suppose in the experts at Atos' eyes. Teaching LB the time has been an ongoing process for the last 2/3 years and no, the boy ain't cracked it yet. Let's park that (minor) detail for now. Do Atos mean a manual alarm clock, where you have to scooby round some second set of hands to the time you want the alarm to go off? Never an easy task. Or a digital alarm clock??? It is ill-thought-out nonsense.

It is murky. It is troubling and troublesome. It is time-consuming and energy-sapping, and it underlines how our children do not fit and, no matter what efforts we make, sit outside the boundaries of what is acceptable.

Did I wash the strawberries when I was pregnant?

Guilt and self-blame are weighty objects in the mother's toolkit and can kick in before and after a child is diagnosed. This is almost inevitable given the negative framing of this process, as we saw in Chapter 3. Nicki summarized this roller-coaster ride of emotions, self-doubt and devastation along with a good dose of self-blame:

Yes. I struggled. I really struggled. I felt guilt. Should I have insisted on a Caesarean? Should I have let the labour go on for three days? I thought did I wash strawberries when I was pregnant? I ate brie, heavens was that it? Mark considered for a while that it might be the jab. And we were both really looking for something or someone to blame. As a mother, my own private thoughts were awful for a while. I thought, you know, how could I possibly exchange Tyler for a normal child? Is there a way I can do that? Extremes. Real extremes. And then feeling guilty because I had thought it and then being really desperate within myself thinking how can I ever protect him? How can I make sure he grows into adulthood? Is he going to have an independent life? I don't want a disabled child. I want a normal child. And all those emotions were an absolute roller-coaster for me. And probably if I am honest lasted about eighteen months and when he was diagnosed I burst into tears and...but I knew that that was what the diagnosis was going to be. I knew it. We knew it.

In addition to self-blame, some mothers feel, or are explicitly, blamed by professionals for their children's developmental delay or difference along the road to diagnosis. Two mothers in the Healthtalk project were labelled with Munchausen by proxy (now called factitious disorder) before their children were diagnosed with autism. To have your expertise and knowledge dismissed and be accused of trying to harm your child is monstrous. The tentacles of mother blame stretch beyond diagnosis, however, as pointing fingers at 'the mother' or 'mum' seems to be a default position. I have experienced it routinely over the four or five years after Connor's death, and knowing many other mothers with similar experiences, I can say with confidence that it is a nasty and debilitating technique and one that should be called out and erased.

Parental health and wellbeing

We know that parents of disabled children experience lower levels of wellbeing than those of non-disabled children,[5] and it is difficult to disentangle disadvantages associated with lower social class, learning disability and the wellbeing of parents.[6] I have no idea what the actual numbers are and am not sure there is research here, but the number of parents on antidepressant medication must be pretty substantial. Liz, a full-time carer when I interviewed her, lived with her husband, a chicken farmer, and two sons aged 11 and eight. The oldest was diagnosed with epilepsy aged seven and attention deficit hyperactivity disorder and Asperger syndrome a year later. Liz was struck by how many parents involved in her local support group were on medication:

> A lot of the parents are very overwhelmed and I certainly have been very overwhelmed and the only way I go forward with it is I am on antidepressants and that was one of the questions we did ask our parents, 'How many parents were on antidepressants just to cope in our everyday life?' And everybody put their hand up. At some point or other they had been on antidepressants. Normally you know if you have got a problem you try to solve problems, but our children's situation is an ongoing thing, so it is not going to go away from one day to the other. So it is the fact that you have that sort of worry and that sort of fight for everything constantly. So unfortunately having to go on antidepressants is one way of keeping you sort of stable, because otherwise you would just crack up basically.

The pressures can be immense and generated by myriad sources including trying to keep family life going on an even keel in what can be a hostile, shifting and challenging environment. Bear in mind, too, that I am not covering education in this book, which is a whole other ocean of stress and active involvement for parents. Again, the dependency work falls disproportionately on mothers, and Liz highlights how she simply has to keep going:

> All those things have got a lot worse than they were before. So it is affecting my health as well and if I am not well, this family would be in bits really, because my husband can't cope with it either. So yes, I have to keep, I think it is the fact that you have

to keep on, you know I am not allowed to be ill. When I am ill everybody is like oh what am I going to do? And sometimes I might have a migraine and I still have to get up and still have to do things because they are not self-sufficient so, yes.

Many mothers describe the importance of trying to remain calm, and there is a commonly used trope about swans and paddling feet below an apparently calm surface. We recognize how being visibly tense and upset benefits no one. Children can sense anxiety and it can have a knock-on impact on family members. Rachel talked about training herself to be calm, and this is what we do. We learn how to marshal good times and head off potentially negative instances. We learn ways of reducing stress and anxiety within the home and when we are out and about. Always walking the tightrope between trying to gain or maintain a measure of social acceptance while fighting for space for what is normal for us.

This unremitting and unsupported work can have a knock-on effect on relationships, as evidenced by the statistics around single-parent families with disabled children. Long days, little external support and a complexity involving dependency work, exhaustion, children not sleeping or sleeping in their parents' bed, the importance of remaining calm and so much more can make it tricky, if not impossible, not to take out frustrations on each other at times, as Amanda notes:

It puts you under a lot of pressure. You know. I mean me and [husband] we find it hard. You never get a minute. It is like you are up in the night with them often. Louis sleeps in my bed most nights. He starts off in his own but by about 2 o'clock he comes teetering through and [husband] just gets out and goes and gets in his bed. He has given up I think. You are under a lot of pressure all the time and you know you have got to try and keep calm with the kids, because if you lose it with them you know, you are just not going to get anywhere. So you know, you do find you snap at each other a little bit and you don't have a lot of time for the marriage as a couple.

Thinking ahead

A further layer of pressure and stress involves worry about the future. I can remember trying to focus on the here and now and firmly park future thoughts when Connor was very young; and then every so often either I or a mum mate would break ranks and express deep concerns that we all seemed to share. I return to this topic in Chapter 7 which discusses the experiences of older carers. It is ever-present even in the earlier years when the children are tiny. A time when thoughts of adulthood should be a flicker in the future. Jane raised this as a concern before her son had started school:

> It concerns me especially about what will happen to [him] when we die. It's quite morbid to think about but it does, it does really concern me. It does worry me, because even though he is little now, you still think about it, because with my other child, I know that I am teaching her now and she is going to be able to take care of herself, and she is going to be able to work and have children and get married and things like that. But he is not going to have those options open and you know, we already know that he is going to need some great deal of care throughout his life. So it does sort of worry me because I don't want him to end up in an institution. I want him to be happy and feel like he can live independently when we do pass away. That worries me.

Amanda similarly said:

> But I have had to accept that they are how they are, you know and I worry about the future you know. I know I should probably just focus on now, but I do worry about what the future holds for them. You know, and them coming into being adolescent and adults that is quite scary.

There is clearly something deeply wrong in the organization and delivery of health and social care (and wider society) when parents of very young children dread their future. It is even more chilling that this does not seem to be on the political or social care agenda – or even on the radar.

Activism, advocacy and support groups

Alongside blame and guilt, the mother's toolkit often contains the ingredients for advocacy and activism. While advocacy is a task most parents undertake, for mothers of disabled children it can develop into something more substantial and enduring. This can begin with attending support groups and gaining knowledge from the experience of other parents and, crucially, meeting other people with similar experiences. While there are not always local support groups available (some parents describe setting up their own), these can be an important resource for many parents. Amanda describes her local support group as a turning point:

> The group, the group I go to [support group] that were a real turning point, because I have got somewhere I can go and talk to people. You know. I think without that, I think if you didn't have that sort of network of support, you would just feel isolated.

It can feel reassuring and comfortable hanging out with families with similar experiences, and strong friendships can develop through these groups as you can laugh, cry, plot and chuckle together. The coming together of sympathetic others can be liberating, warming and productive as Liz comments:

> And I would just say to anybody with a newly diagnosed child is you know, I mean it is not everybody's cup of tea going to support groups, but just don't be alone with it. You know. Go and talk to people, get out there. You know. You might think that you can't take your child anywhere but if you go with a group then you know they do organize trips and things and you can go and you realize that you are not on your own. There is other parents and you will make some friends. There is other parents going through the same. You know I mean without [support group] I probably would be not as calm as I am today because it is just, they are at the end of the phone if you need some advice, they are at the end of the phone.

In addition to providing peer support, these groups can develop a campaign focus as the seeds of injustice in terms of the health, social care and education opportunities and services offered to our children become clearer when shared. The scrutiny and surveillance families often feel under can also lead to an element of resistance. Nicki describes how her group campaigns for local change:

> I help run a parents support group for parents of children with autism and Asperger's and as part of that we had a representative from the Council come who is responsible for the leisure strategy and we were very keen to put forward our views as parents that there is very little in terms of special educational needs leisure facilities. There's no holiday clubs for children with special needs, there is nothing like that. A lot of the pools have split changing rooms and no family changing rooms which means that once Tyler becomes eight, he needs to go into a changing room on his own. That is just not possible. He just won't do it. He will get distracted. It won't be that he can't do it, it will be that he will be in there and he will wander round and he will think oh showers great fun and stand in the shower.

Jane similarly described how becoming involved in a support group has led to her campaigning with other local parents for improved local services. She clearly found this activist work satisfying and empowering, an important strand of activity for some parents who are not able to undertake paid employment because of child-caring responsibilities:

> At first I joined our local support group and it has got over a hundred members and I met quite a few people through there, good friends through there that have really helped me and explained things. But I have taken, from that support group I have joined up with three other groups and we are campaigning for services locally to be improved. And I really like that aspect of it because…something positive has come out of it. It is something positive that I can do. I don't, we don't sit around moaning about our child's condition, what they can do, we do something really positive to improve the chances they have in life.

Mike, who ran a very active support group in the north of England, said that professionals can feel intimidated by parent groups and feel they are going to be attacked. It can be difficult for parents to remain measured and calm in these settings at times, and a combination of parental love, emotion and grim determination can generate a less than helpful response from professionals present.

I remember being warned off parent groups by a psychologist when Connor was tiny. He dismissed them as 'a bunch of moaning minnies'. This is in contrast to another mother who tweeted how she was actively encouraged to meet other families:

> When A was 3 months old & recently diagnosed, our specialist health visitor arranged for us to start at child devt centre on same day as another family, saying 'I think you will get on well'. 23yrs later our kids and families are still best of friends, and mutual lifelines. (Liz Elston@lizogradyelston)

My experience of activism began when Connor was a tot, meeting other parents and the development of lifelong friendships and strong activist roots. We all still look back with a wry fondness for those early experiences which generated bonds, humour and collective aims. I'm not sure the council were anticipating the oomph we packed as we plotted and planned campaigns and strategies, and I imagine this kind of work was and still is replicated across the country. Parents have always been, unsurprisingly, key champions for social change. You only have to look at the genesis of big charities such as Mencap and the National Austistic Society, set up by parent campaigners, to see what empowered and dedicated parents can achieve.

Some years back, Katherine Runswick-Cole and I wrote about advocacy and activism, drawing on an analysis of the Healthtalk data.[7] We puzzled over what made some parents tip into an explicitly activist role while others adopted more internal activism, and eventually we decided a continuum was a useful way of better understanding this:

This continuum is a useful heuristic device because of the advocacy role most mothers assume during their children's lives whether or not their children are disabled. A continuum also allows for movements in both directions allowing mothers to reduce their activist role at certain points in their lives, thus incorporating the few parents who described 'lapsing' in their involvement with support groups and campaigning and allowing for changing circumstances across the life course.[8]

In our analysis we found around half the mothers did not attend support groups or extend their advocacy role. The mothers who did described finding activism satisfying and rewarding; it extended their professionalism and their understanding of complex social systems on behalf of their own child or children and others.

The development of social media since we wrote this paper has revolutionized the ease and accessibility for (some) parents to hook up and collectively engage on different platforms such as Twitter, Instagram and Facebook. Sadly, there are stories of parents' social media activity being the space of further surveillance by NHS Trusts and local authorities. Health and social care need to embrace the opportunities these platforms allow people to make and use the discussions and issues raised interactively to learn and improve practice.

So what is the learning here for health and social care professionals? How can parents and professionals work together to improve the experiences for families? Working with parent or self-advocacy/campaign groups is a clear win in terms of trying to improve the provision of health and social care. Public and patient involvement is an established feature in the health and social care research landscape. Working with a bunch of activated, committed and dedicated parents is too often an untapped resource for professionals. We are prepared to put in hours of (unpaid) labour for our own and other children.

This 'working with' must be treated with respect and decency, however. I have lost count of the number of meetings I have attended over the years with various professionals where we have not even been offered travel expenses. There is often little recognition of the mountains moved to attend, or how a precious break from childcare is being gifted to professionals. Families should be treated as equal partners in this work, and it is important that the levels of dependency work being conducted are recognized and thought about in terms of the timing and location of meetings. There needs to be recognition of the resources parents are drawing on to attend. Try to imagine what it must be like to live in fear of the future while juggling numerous balls of bureaucratic demands, childcare and wider family life, while still pitching up to meetings in the hope of pushing through change.

'Sometimes it's the little things'

I've always been struck by how many health and social care professionals can appear blinkered to some of the demands families face, and ignore so much of the work they do. A friend of mine used a hoist with her daughter at home, on her own, for years and was devastated when a much-anticipated activity her daughter loved which would give her a brief break, such as a swimming session, was cancelled because not enough staff were available to safely hoist her. This lack of recognition or acknowledgement of the sometimes physical and medical labour undertaken by families, in particular mothers, can add to feelings of isolation.

It is very much within the gift of health and social care professionals to reassure parents that they are doing a good job but it does not seem to happen frequently. This is even more so when the child has become an adult, school is ending and the future looks bleak:

When I asked the head teacher in my son's post-16 unit whether I was being unreasonable thinking he needed a specialist further ed college & she said I was the most reasonable person she'd ever met. (Red Queen – @Wythanie)

The educational psychologist who said 'no, you are not being unreasonable' when everyone else seemed to be saying the opposite & I was losing faith in my own judgement. Sometimes it is the little things. (Katherine Runswick-Cole – @K_Runswick_Cole)

Postscript

My fingers have itched at times writing this chapter because it involves page after page detailing grim experiences, a litany of challenges and the gut-wrenching hard work that parents, in particular mothers, do. It would be disingenuous to brush over this labour or downplay it, because it can be bloody hard. However, the difficulty is to a large extent because of the lack of services and support and a looming black hole when thinking ahead. The incredible joy and intensity of love and pride we feel about our children is extraordinary, and the ways in which we learn from them is something that we (all – dare I make this claim?) hold on to. Eva Kittay deserves the last say in this chapter:

> The young woman who is my daughter will never read a book of philosophy – she will never read – and will never speak English sentences. She will never be independent. The lessons of this book, nonetheless, are the product of her gentle tutoring. The lessons are not over and will continue as long as we have each other. The process of mothering will not end, just as marriages are not supposed to end 'till death do us part'. Until then, I will continue to learn from my daughter, from those who share her mothering with me, and from the unique and at times also generalizable, aspects of this remarkable relationship with an exquisite person we call Sesha.[9]

Chapter 6

Becoming an Adult

We have seen across earlier chapters that adulthood casts a dark cloud across childhood for families with disabled children.

We know that adult services for learning-disabled and/or autistic people are often mediocre or non-existent. We spend years worrying, consciously or unconsciously, about what the enormity of a future without imagination, aspiration, appropriate support or shape might look like, and, all too soon it seems, that moment arrives. For many parents, this substitutes battles about education provision with new scripts and different words, individuals, jargon, rules and bafflement. It even kicks off with a word that may as well have flashing lights and alarm bells hanging off it. *Transition*. A word that works to separate out the expectations and aspirations experienced by most children from those who are denied this. Talking about 'transition' creates a different space to leave childhood with a differently shaped adulthood to enter.

Connor's sister and brothers meandered through school and university (eventually), knuckled down in various ways, had fun with mates and relationships, and got on with it. They grew older, supported in becoming adults by those around them: family, friends, peers, teachers, employees and other people they came into contact with. In contrast, Connor (and I) had a set of formal and bleak meetings with various professionals we had never met before and who knew nothing about him or our family.

This is a key point in young people's lives, and it seems to be one that social care professionals can get very wrong. This is, in part, because they may be facing formidable/fearful/weary parents who have undertaken nearly two decades of dependency work and advocacy, and who may have been let down along the way. Parents with advocacy underpinned by fierce and intense love. This may be daunting for professionals, especially given that little appropriate support to enable people to lead flourishing lives is too often lacking. Emotions may run high as our fears of no apparent future materialize.

Various reforms and policies highlight the existence of this black hole. For example, the extension of the scope of Education Health and Care* (EHC) plans to the age of 25 and the publication in 2015 of 'Building the Right Support',[1] a national programme that aims to improve the lives of learning-disabled people by supporting them to live in their own homes. The drag continues to drag, however. A conversation with a mate while writing this illustrated how little has changed since Connor turned 18, six years ago now. This friend's 17-year-old son has two more years at school, then the possibility of two colleges (neither particularly appropriate) in different parts of the country, with mystery surrounding how a college place might be funded. The alternative is for his son to live at home, with either his mum or dad 'looking after him'. This is the current state of provision in the UK.

It is almost ironic that this is a time in which the knowledge and agency of family, friends and significant others in the lives of young people is so important, and yet it is at this point that families can be distanced and dismissed.

It is crucially important that the period approaching adulthood is treated as a space of potential possibilities by professionals. Despite the introduction of different initiatives such as direct payments, personal budgets and 'person-centred care', the countdown to adulthood remains too often a barren terrain for young people and their families, dotted with rocky outcrops and few or no signs of the green shoots of growth and new life. The

---

*   www.ipsea.org.uk/pages/category/education-health-and-care-plans

lives and adulthoods of young learning-disabled and/or autistic people are as important as those of any other young people.

Connor and transitions

The most generous interpretation of our experience of 'transition' was lacklustre or just lacking. When Connor was about 14 or 15, a social worker popped up at his annual review. She came to our house a year or so later to fill in a form, with Connor about to become an adult. I remember there was space to fill in three things he liked. With much prompting, Connor said 'lorries', then 'lorries' and 'lorries'. An adult social worker later appeared and talked budgets and panel. There was no discussion about what Connor might like to do or be when he left school, what sort of job or training. How we might support him in doing this. It was a form-filling and filing exercise. There are few obvious options, social workers are stretched, and there is little in the way of good examples to point to. Imagination, if it ever existed, has been stifled by years of austerity.

The kids and their mates became more forward-thinking and focused in their late teens, heading out to pubs and clubs, talking about university or jobs. Rosie went to university in Manchester, Will stopped coming over so often as he took on a labouring job near Reading, and the shape of our family began to change. Connor's future remained unstructured and bleak. There was no university or job to apply for, and I'm sure he was able to tap into the stress and concern about this abyss. His head teacher (now retired) always thought his deepening anxiety and distress related in part to having older siblings who were striking out into the world in a way denied to him. They had opportunity and choices in abundance, while his future was restricted to staying at school for an additional two years and little beyond that. Having spent his childhood as part of a pack of lively children including his sister, brothers, their friends and neighbours, he was used to fun and laughter. Looking back now, I can see how he seamlessly drifted in and out, taking himself off to his room or the garden to read a book, listen to his music or watch YouTube videos, enjoying the banter, the love, the hanging out, while living on his own terms. This was steadily and systematically changing.

Connor's immediate future was such a concern that I drummed up the idea of setting up a social enterprise to try to draw on his strengths. Connor was a big supporter of recycling and had enjoyed working as an assistant caretaker at his school for a couple of years, picking up litter in the playing field during breaks. He was meticulous in this work, fully absorbed, engaged, and it gave him satisfaction to do the task well. The plan was to get a small van with a mobile paper shredder in the back and work up a route to park up locally, taking in residential areas and the odd small business park. Connor would be the key shredder because of his skills in this area, and one or more of his more gregarious classmates would be the front face of the gig, meeting and greeting the punters to collect the work. I could see this idea generating actual employment for two or three young people as well as providing a practical and social service for the local community. We would get the van on the road for a few days a week to begin with and see how it went. The problem was I had no idea how to go about organizing this and what it meant for the mystery (and misery) surrounding 'panel' and 'indicative budgets'. I was in the process of visiting other social enterprise schemes when Connor went downhill.

Transitions today – budgets and more

So where are we now? There have been what can be important changes to the organization of social care, with the introduction of personal budgets and self-directed support.[2] Personal budgets are, in theory, supposed to offer people more independence and choice in their adult lives (and childhood), and, in principle, these payments can be used as part of an EHC plan. This is not a panacea, however, as choice is an empty concept when there is nothing to choose between. In addition, the management of personal budgets and direct payments can be burdensome (see

Mark Neary's blog* for meticulous accounts of the work involved in these processes). In addition, there is no magic staff tree for families to shake. Finding and keeping good staff can be a pretty onerous and stressful task. It can too often be a one-way gig, with local authorities and the government quick to enforce deadlines and demands while acting with bone-crushing slowness when it comes to taking action themselves.

Independent supported living

The most recent figures,† which again show substantial variation across local authorities, suggest that council-managed budgets are the most common social care support that learning-disabled adults are receiving, council-commissioned community support continues to decrease, and 19% of all learning-disabled adults aged 18–64 are in residential and nursing care, 37% of people aged 18–64 live at home with their families, while 22% of working-age adults live in some form of supported living. This typically involves living in a shared house in communities with support workers on a rota for a certain number of hours per person. Some independent supported living places have 24-hour care, and this should depend on what sort of support is needed by the people who live there. The underlying principle of independent supported living is that the person has the choice of where to live and who provides the support for them. People should also be able to choose who they live with, like most people. In practice, these choices are very limited.

There are further issues around independent supported living which seem to be worsening. A Radio 4 *File on Four* programme, *No Place Like Home*,[3] which aired in early 2019, found that there has been a 40% increase in the number of unexpected deaths and a 279% increase in serious injury over the previous eight

---

*   https://markneary1dotcom1.wordpress.com
†   The collecting of social care data is not brilliant in the UK, and I would recommend Professor Chris Hatton's blog – https://chrishatton.blogspot.com/2019/10/social-care-statistics-and-adults-with.html – for up-to-date analysis and commentary.

years. While this increase could, in part, be due to an increase in numbers of people living in supported living and better reporting of serious injuries and death, it is unlikely. Jayne Knight, an independent consultant who featured on the programme, reported an estimated 20–30% of homes providing good care in line with the Reach[4] standards (see box) and 60% falling far short of this.

Reach standards

1. I choose who I live with

2. I choose where I live

3. I have my own home

4. I choose how I am supported

5. I choose who supports me

6. I get good support

7. I choose my friends and relationships

8. I choose how to be healthy and safe

9. I choose how I am part of the community

10. I have the same rights and responsibilities as other citizens

11. I get help to make changes in my life

The problem seems to be, in part, one of money, or lack of money, as the social care budget has been decimated in England. When people lived in residential settings, the local authorities footed the full bill. In supported living, people become tenants in their homes and their rent is covered by Housing Benefit which is centrally paid. This has led to local authorities encouraging people to move into independent supported living when it may not be appropriate for them. There is also a downgrading of people's support needs which allows fewer staff to be on duty. As *No Place Like Home* reported, staff ratios can be so low that if one person needs to attend a GP appointment, everyone in the house has to go. This clearly flies in the face of choice, independence and autonomy. A further layer of complexity and concern is that the CQC cannot inspect people's homes and so inspections focus on the provider's head office, with only one or two homes visited (if at all). This means poor care can go unrecognized for long periods of time.

A recent study looked at the quality of life that learning-disabled people experience living in the community and focused on evening routines.[5] The Big Bedtime Audit involved visiting 56 settings managed by 28 care-provider organizations across two local authorities with 313 people living in them. Sixty-nine per cent of people living in these settings were engaged in a bedtime-related activity by 8.30pm. The pervasiveness of institutional regimes in apparently 'independent supported living' settings is chilling and too often goes under the radar. The research team described finding a note pinned to the chair of one person which stated:

> Dinner 5pm; Bedtime 6pm; With Medication; Night Night; Sweet Dreams.[6]

As chillingly, not enough staff on duty led to another person being 'padded up in case of incident'.[7] The authors of this study, experienced senior social workers/commissioners, commented on Twitter that they were not surprised by the findings.

A regulatory affair: Cherry Tree and the CQC

The CQC 'monitor, inspect and regulate services to make sure they meet fundamental standards of quality and safety' and publish performance ratings to help people choose care.[8] Five domains guide inspections: safety, effectiveness, leadership, responsiveness and caring. The inspection focus is largely on basic care rather than the aspirational criteria essential to leading a happy and full life. This is underlined by a recent case in which the CQC was taken to court by a service provider called Care Management Group (CMG). It is an illuminating and depressing example of how low the bar of what is considered to be acceptable support and care is in reality.[9]

In April 2017, the CQC refused an application from a private care provider, CMG, to extend the number of 'beds' from seven to ten in a property called Cherry Tree which is located on a campus-type site with other houses run by the same provider. The CQC proposed to refuse the application because it did not comply with the 'Registering the Right Support'[10] policy. The reasons given included: the proposed extension was not compliant with the Health and Social Care Act; Cherry Tree is part of a campus-style setting which is against national guidance; no evidence was provided to demonstrate that the expansion was required; there was no evidence of compelling reasons why the CQC should depart from their guidance; and the CQC was not assured that appropriate consultation with people living at the site, families or the local commissioners to identify local need had taken place. The full decision is worth a careful read to see the construction of the arguments that the CMG legal representative made to persuade the judge that this extension was needed. These arguments included the statement that refusing this bed expansion would deny future users the opportunity to choose to live in the service provided by a regulated provider who provides good care in this venue'.[11] Breath-taking complacency as it turned out.

The tribunal panel members, who were clearly a sensible bunch, went to visit Cherry Tree during the hearing. From the off they were able to clearly see serious deficiencies and limitations in the support provided that had not been apparent to the CQC inspectors. The house had to be accessed along an unlit lane which took around seven minutes on foot from the road, with a few hundred feet further to reach the bus stop in either direction on the road. This clearly militated against any sense of community connectedness and was potentially risky, particularly in the evening. An unusually high fence around the properties on the site reminded the panel of a young offenders institution, rather than someone's home. CMG said this was due to the propensity for one person to try to do a bunk, even though, as the judge noted, the apparent one-to-one support meant this should not be an issue. There is so much so wrong in the detail of this hearing that I will include one, lengthy, extract here which examines the opportunities the people who live at Cherry Tree have to interact with other people. CMG had argued that the increase in the number of people living at Cherry Tree would benefit the house in terms of additional people to interact with:

> However, Dr Joyce's [expert witness] overarching point was that it is not normal to have to live with others in order to enjoy the benefits of relationships/interaction. We agree. The opportunities for social interaction are obviously increased if people with autism and behaviour that challenges live within and are part of ordinary communities where, if they choose, the benefits of a diverse range of social interaction can be more easily enjoyed.[12]

CMG are using 'insane' arguments here. The number of beds in a supported living house should not be extended to provide people living there with an increased opportunity for social interaction. Making this argument completely discredits the provider's claim to provide good care. The judge continued:

> It is an odd feature of the evidence that much emphasis was placed by Ms Dodgson and Ms Molineux upon the fact that the service users in the different buildings are effectively kept separate, except for occasional social events such as barbeques. This is odd in the context that one part of the Appellant's case is that RB and JT would benefit from socialisation with others. It was also odd because the evidence as to why the different groups of service users are effectively kept apart was different. Ms Dodgson said it was because of compatibility issues. Ms Molineux said it was because of training needs: i.e. the carers assigned to each service users may not be able to cope with the needs of another service user. If the latter is accurate, it reflects a very narrow approach to person centred care. We found that both explanations were unsatisfactory and inconsistent with the

Appellant's case that JT and RB would benefit from socialisation that, on any basis, the provider has sought to limit across the setting as a whole. Both JT and RB had been at Cherry Tree for approaching 2 years before the application was made. Overall the evidence about the different groups of service users being kept apart or separate in the setting we find exists, illuminates the clear risks of isolation: both from the community outside and even within the community within the setting.[13]

The CQC was spot on in refusing to allow CMG to expand the size of the provision. There were no grounds to do so, despite the trumped-up reasons provided. However, this judgement also underlines how the CQC inspection regime is based on a narrow set of criteria which does not capture the bigger picture of exclusion, bleakness and the absence of any attempts to enable people to lead flourishing lives.

Another care home up north received a good CQC rating recently because residents (shudder) were clean and well fed. This is despite 19 people living in the home and only around two staff on duty across the day and night. The low staffing levels meant that people were unable to go out into their community to do the things most of us take for granted. Being clean, well fed and safe underpins but does not equate to a flourishing life.

Flourishing lives

Some of Connor's classmates now live in a house that one of the families built opposite the primary school they all attended in a village outside Oxford. The house backs on to fields and is a short walk along a footpath from the shops and pubs and the bus stop into Oxford. Support workers are employed by a good and smallish Oxfordshire provider, and family and friends drop in all the time. They are leading busy, full and fun lives, going out and about, hanging out, attending events and cooking.

There is a sense of connectedness about their lives which is in part due to the way in which schoolchildren from the primary and secondary school have, for years, been involved in village life. We have numerous photos of Connor sweeping the churchyard, working in the local pub, shopping in Asda for meal prep ingredients, or just going for a walk around the village. Some ex-pupils now work in Asda. There is a comfortable familiarity and buzz around the whole shebang.

This is, in no small part, because of the hands-on work of their parents who have been determined to help generate fulfilling lives for their children. Not everyone has family members to support them and/or the resources to set up something like this. It is also not without its problems. There is no reason, however, why people can't lead similarly full lives, and questions really should be asked and followed up about those who are not.

Another young man living a good life is Christian Raphael who has a blog brilliantly named 'Pubs and Gigs and Cakes'.* Christian started the blog a year or so ago and it documents a whirlwind of fun stuff, love, family life and politics with the occasional dip into hospital through health complications:

> Starting out on my third decade, spent my twenties hitting brick walls and banging on doors to change health outcomes and inclusion with people with learning disabilities. Now a new chapter, a blog written by and with me, my PAs and family and friends. It will start with pubs, gigs and cake but will lead us to who knows where.

These examples of showing how life can be are priceless, and yet too often come with a price attached as it is the resources families have or are able to draw upon, rather than available support and services, that generate the necessary conditions to flourish.

The world of work

Work is a central feature of being human. It involves being productive, earning, contributing, having structure in our lives

---

*   https://pubsandgigsandcake.weebly.com

and opportunities to interact with people. We know that a tiny number of learning-disabled people are in paid employment and an estimated 65% of learning-disabled people would like to work.[14] We are incredibly poor in the UK at supporting people to work or even having aspirations to work.

There are exceptions, of course. The Foxes Hotel* in Minehead is the only fully operating training hotel for learning-disabled adults in the UK. The Foxes Academy attached to the hotel has an outstanding Ofsted rating with an 86% employment rating for graduates (43% of whom are paid). Some third-sector organizations also work to support people. Oxford-based charity Yellow Submarine† aims to offer young people a stepping-stone to independence with thriving cafés in Oxford and Witney. These social enterprise cafés offer training opportunities for people to learn catering skills on the job, and the organization supports young people in jobs locally. These drops of brilliance, however, are few and far between.

I remember reading about Michael Edwards, one of the founders of My Life My Choice, a self-advocacy group in Oxford when Connor was a tot. I had not come across the charity before and was chilled by Michael's description of his experience of 'sorting plastics' in what used to be called Adult Training Facilities. The unpaid work involved sorting different-shaped plastics into trays. If he and his colleagues finished sorting them before the end of the day, the supervisor would simply tip the boxes out so they could be sorted again. The utter futility of this task was so harrowing I never forgot the article.[15]

Volunteering – in this context an alternative to sorting plastics – is seen by some as a stepping-stone to work or alternative employment, although research suggests that volunteering alone is unlikely to lead to employment.[16] A Canadian study of

---

* https://foxeshotel.co.uk
† www.yellowsubmarine.org.uk

the experiences of a supported employment scheme suggested that the goal for some learning-disabled people should be 'meaningful activity' rather than paid employment.[17] This takes us dangerously close to calls over the years to allow people to earn less than the minimum wage[18] – a call that recently reared its inappropriate head as an MP stated that learning-disabled people should be paid less than the minimum wage because they didn't understand money.[19]

Instead of downgrading the contributions learning-disabled and/or autistic people can make in paid employment to fluff, made-up jobs or exploitation, we should be critically reformulating assumptions of what constitutes 'ability' and create working environments in which we can all contribute. The denial of work opportunities to so many young people and adults who could work with support and thoughtfulness is wrong. As I write this, My Life My Choice have just launched their 'Walk it like you talk it' campaign that encourages companies to employ a minimum of 1% staff with learning disabilities. Leading and showing the way forward.

Fun and loving

Fun and love are too often absent from social care considerations and thinking, and yet are, or should be, a central feature in people's lives.

* * * * *

A brilliant development over the last few years began with a punk band Heavy Load and recognition that people were leaving their gigs at 9pm because support workers want people home by 10pm. The charity Stay Up Late* was established and from this Gig Buddies† was hatched. Stay Up Late ripped through the idea that learning-disabled/and or autistic people can't be out

*   https://stayuplate.org
†   www.gigbuddies.org.uk

after 8.30pm because of support-related issues, and Gig Buddies offered a mechanism to sort this out. The organization, set up by Paul Richards, has dripped cool from the start and is now being franchised across England. It's a simple idea: people volunteer to be 'gig buddies' and are matched with people based on similar interests – gigs, meals out, theatre and so on. A win-win situation with the potential to become embedded across the country. Let's hope it will make a dent in the tendency for people to be put to bed early.

Another piece of brilliance (again my fingers are heavy on the keyboard typing about 'initiatives around having fun and love...') is Supported Loving* run by Choice Support. Supported Loving was started by Dr Clare Bates after her PhD research found that people wanted loving relationships (no big reveal) but were dependent on being supported by staff to start and continue these.[20] Supported Loving aims to ensure that sexuality and relationships are a mandatory focus in CQC inspections, that all social care staff have training on sexuality and relationships, and that people are aware of their sexual rights.

Dipping into CQC inspection reports can make your heart sink when you read about how providers are doing very little or nothing to support friendships or intimate relationships – indeed, some places work to erase both. Several learning-disabled friends talk about how lonely they feel and how they would love to be in a relationship. The Channel 4 programme *Undateables*† did a reasonable job here, despite controversy over the title of the show. It presented different people each week being supported to go on dates, often with the help of specialist dating agencies, and captured people's hopes and dreams, humour and the interaction between family members in a warm and thoughtful way.

A BBC Radio 4 programme *Assisted Loving*‡ was aired in December 2019, presented by Sui-Ling Tang, a learning-disabled woman in her 40s. Sui-Ling is engaged to Lloyd who she had a

* www.choicesupport.org.uk/about-us/what-we-do/supported-loving
† www.channel4.com/programmes/the-undateables
‡ www.bbc.co.uk/programmes/m000c4vh

crush on in school and met again years later at a bus stop. The programme also featured Clare Bates and a set of mothers from Yorkshire who talked about their hopes and fears in terms of the future love lives of their daughters and sons. Sui-Ling smashed the programme with her characteristic forthrightness and sharp wit, which was an antidote to some of the sadder aspects covered: a fear of certain people having sex and intimate relationships, and the lack of support available to enable these.

A brief dip into fiction and non-fiction

We will take a diversion here to reflect on three books that should be essential reading for health and social care students and professionals: *Riding the Bus with My Sister* by Rachel Simon,[21] *Scapegoat* by Katherine Quarmby[22] and *Flowers for Algernon* by Daniel Keyes.[23]

In *Riding the Bus with My Sister*, Rachel, an author, is concerned that her sister, Beth, is both putting herself at risk and wasting her time riding the buses in a Pennsylvania city all day, every day. At Beth's request, Rachel spends a year riding the bus with her, and the book is an account of this year. As time goes on, Rachel begins to both recognize and understand the elaborate layers and relationships that Beth has woven in doing this activity. Rachel learned over the course of the year that, economically, Beth was better off riding the buses than doing a piecemeal job because of the way the benefit system worked. Socially, Beth had developed a network of friendly bus drivers and other passengers and was astutely avoiding drivers who were less friendly. By the end of the year, Rachel not only better understood Beth's life but also began to recognize limitations in her own.

It can take a stern pulling-up to not make judgements about people's actions and choices, particularly if they seem risky and pointless. It comes back to the importance of co-mingling and just hanging out with people that I discussed in Chapter 1.

I bought a copy of Katherine Quarmby's book *Scapegoat* a while back and couldn't read beyond the introduction for a good year or so. I felt physically sick at the terror, pain and cruelty people have been subjected to for no other reason than being perceived to be different. Quarmby, a journalist, investigated various hate crimes across the UK, documenting one harrowing case after another.

Just one example is Sean Miles, a 37-year-old autistic man who lived in Oxford. He was tortured and then drowned by a group of three people who lived near him.[24] Sentencing all three to life, the judge said: 'This was a particularly heartless and cruel murder. Your victim was extremely vulnerable with a very low IQ, autistic, disadvantaged and thought anyone who spoke to him was his friend.'

The judge drew attention to one of the factors that always stops me in my tracks:

> Each of you played a part in that. Not one of you lifted a finger to help him, nor did you summon help, nor did you report him missing.

Thinking back to Ely Hospital, to Winterbourne View, to Whorlton Hall, Mendip House[25] and other scandals, it is the bystanders who chill me as much as the perpetrators. The fact that it takes 'fresh eyes' and an understanding of being human, like Mr Pantilledes, like Terry Bryan, to call out these crimes is baffling.

The examples Quarmby details are barbaric, and it is hard not to conclude that certain people are somehow seen as fair game for such cruelty, in part because they are less likely to be able to defend themselves or tell other people (or be listened to). Quarmby similarly concludes that 'the targeting of disabled people has happened while society has looked the other way'.[26] These crimes are condoned by society in a type of collective culpability; they happen in front of us, with few people stepping in or stepping up to stop them. These crimes are also an extreme manifestation of inclusion phobia. A marking out and deliberate and cruel targeting of difference.

Finally, a turn to fiction with *Flowers for Algernon*. Written by Daniel Keyes and published originally in 1965, the story is narrated by Charlie Gordon, a learning-disabled factory worker. Gordon is the first person to receive an experimental drug to make him more 'clever'. The drug is first used on a mouse called Algernon. The idea for the story came, in part, from Keyes's experience of working in a special school. A pupil asked if he could get smarter and move to a mainstream class.[27] I don't want to give too much of the story away, but as Charlie starts to understand things more clearly, he begins to recognize how he has been treated over the years. He also tracks the progress of the experiment, keeping Algernon in his flat.

The book packs a deeply uncomfortable, powerful and poignant punch. The unusual storyline reveals much of what remain enduring attitudes towards learning-disabled and/or autistic people.

There have also been significant challenges in the US over the years to censor the book as Charlie tries to make sense of his sexual desires. That fear of promiscuity runs deep.

Podtastic

On a brighter note, I wanted to briefly mention the Challenging Behaviours podcast:*

> Challenging Behaviours is a podcast where Jack, Tom and occasionally Adam aim to challenge behaviours towards disability. The fellas have a wide range of different experience, and talk over a wide range of subjects.

Jack, Tom (hands up that this is our Tom) and Adam met working at a local charity for learning-disabled young people and form a cheerful, thoughtful and engaging trio who gently, and sometimes hilariously, challenge attitudes through discussion with weekly guests. Jack worked extraordinary magic to line up

---

* https://player.fm/series/challenging-behaviours

a brilliant guest list including Sally Phillips, Dr Frances Ryan and RJ Mitte from *Breaking Bad*. The beauty and power of this series is the starting point of the three presenters in treating everyone as human. It is reminiscent, in a way, of the siblings in Chapter 4 who viewed themselves as helping out rather than doing non-normative tasks at home, which researchers seemed to think would cause them lasting damage. The podcast is an exemplar of anti-inclusion phobia positioning without pomp.

What price older parents...

So, what about parents and families in this adult life space? Given the policy rhetoric and focus on choice, autonomy and (supported) independence, someone new to this area might well imagine families are able to back off at this point and leave their adult daughter or son to live their own life with appropriate support from the local authority. Seeing each other socially, hanging out in the different ways families do when children have grown up and are living their own lives.

Unfortunately, this version of what should be is rare in practice. Views on what is considered to be appropriate support will often differ between families and professionals, and families can constantly fear further cuts to services. The pockets of brilliance I know of involve very close involvement with families and layers of dependency work, albeit with a slightly different shape and texture in terms of the tasks and skills involved.

The general lack of opportunities and openings for young people impacts further on parents who can remain restricted in their opportunities for paid employment.

As I write this section on the eve of the December 2019 General Election, a young autistic academic tweeted about how she was genuinely scared about the election result as she felt so vulnerable. Isobel Smith (@lhallsmithSmith), who has been vigilant in trying to protect her son and his partner, now living in independent supported living for decades, replied:

And older parents of adult people with learning disabilities – battle weary – rigid with fear of what is to come if Tory contempt is enabled through stupidity – cuts in our loved one even deeper – a most terrible time to leave them...

By the time children grow into adulthood, their parents may have interrupted their paid working lives for a good 20 years or so. If their children then leave home to move into a supported living set-up, the parents or parent, most typically mother, is left without skills recognized in the paid workplace while also losing Carer's Allowance. Decades of caring get you zero brownie points in the employment market.

...and siblings?

There is little research about family relationships once autistic people reach adulthood.[28] Studies about siblings of learning-disabled adults highlight strong emotional bonds and maintained contact,[29] with some ambivalence.[30] This is pretty much true for most or many adult family relationships over time, with shifting contexts, responsibilities and experiences. Juggling family responsibilities, both immediate and wider, work, household tasks and getting on with life can be demanding. As I mentioned earlier, it can be difficult sifting through research in this area. One study, for example, which seemed to set out to prove how truly awful the impact of having an adult autistic sibling was, concluded: 'Although almost all participants reported some negative aspects, these were mostly balanced by positive experiences as well.'[31] An exemplar of mealy-mouthed, reluctant reporting of findings. In short, a mix of experiences. Peer-reviewed studies woven with underlying assumptions and judgements feed into and help sustain harmful discourses around burden and worthlessness.

Earlier, we saw the mismatch between how siblings help out at home and how this activity can be framed as a pathological undertaking in research and practice. A further study found that adult siblings can experience frustration with professionals as they feel that a lifelong commitment alongside flexibility are 'normal features' of sibling relationships.[32] Two examples of how perceptions and assumptions colour what actually is. While parents run the gauntlet of negotiating space and a measure of acceptance for their children, I suspect siblings (disabled and non-disabled) often just get on with being and doing a lot of the time.

Previous negative experiences with services and support can remain with siblings from childhood. Adult siblings can have low expectations of support and services, and are aware of the precariousness surrounding them. Again, this is no big surprise. Our children develop a sophisticated understanding of the quality and availability of services and support, simply by living through both conversations around this and regular examples of how low it can go.

Recommendations from this research include early engagement with siblings from childhood and the importance of recognizing that 'adult sibling relationships are rooted in past experiences, current circumstances and future expectations'.[33] Once again, we are back to avoiding atomization. You cannot extract one family member and try to deal with that one individual (whether an adult or a child). There are intricately and loosely woven relationships which will shift over time. Other recommendations include noting and sharing sibling details on people's records, pinning down the sort of contact siblings would like on care plans, and asking what support siblings would like from the provider. Such sense and sensibility. Common decency and treating people with respect.

Some siblings or parents will not maintain contact. One Healthtalk participant said she no longer saw her brother because he lived a long way away and she did not see any point. In some cases, siblings may have less than good intentions. One example, as Catherine in her late 60s recounts, from a recent study:

> I don't talk to my sister, well I haven't seen her for ages and I don't want to, well I will tell you why, my brother Tom before he passed away we went to his house, he was in a place, there were

lady carers looking after him day and night and every time I went to see him [with her], she [my sister] wanted him to go to the hole in the wall [ATM] and get money from his money card and when he died she took a lot of things off Tom and they asked me well apparently he left a letter where he got some money, writing letters to me and I never did get that letter so I don't know, I can't do nothing about it because I haven't got the letter [...] when my sister went into his room and took his things I didn't like it and I haven't seen her since.[34]

Self-advocacy

In the previous chapter I discussed parent advocacy and activism. In adulthood, people are often doing it for themselves, and the UK is historically pretty good at this. Although difficult to pin down exactly, self-advocacy is held to have begun in the UK with the setting up of People First London Boroughs in 1984.[35] From that point, it has had feast and famine times as groups proliferated, some funded by local authorities and others independent, and then faded away. It is not clear if these groups are a mechanism for members to develop self-confidence and the skills to speak out, or have a collective function of campaigning for change. There is also criticism that self-advocacy groups struggle to represent people with severe and multiple learning disabilities.[36] Further tension centres on funding and whether independence and the ability to be a critical voice are compromised by local or national government funding.

One of the leading self-advocacy groups in the UK is My Life My Choice which is led by learning-disabled people. In a short film, Michael Edwards describes how:

> We get people to choose for themselves, like housing or whatever. We help them with whatever problems that they have. In the

beginning it was hard work to get people on side but certainly in the last ten years it's improved greatly. I welcome people with open arms. The bigger we are, the better we are going to be and we can do more work and get more funding. Four in the beginning and now 500 and growing. From little acorns the big tree grows. I feel very proud that I started something that is still been going for 18 years and hopefully it will carry on for a long time to come.*

A brief look at their website† shows the range of work the charity undertakes, which includes practical work such as supporting people to travel in their communities, working with NHS Trusts and the CQC to improve services, and campaigning on important issues such as hate crime and #JusticeforLB.

Again, hands up about personal interest‡ as I have worked with the charity for years now and remain in awe of their enthusiasm, kick-ass attitude and generosity.

Dawn Wiltshire and Otto Baxter also feature in the film, Dawn talking about her experience of a group of us walking on the Camino in Northern Spain in memory of Connor and other young people who died preventable deaths:

Last year I went to Spain, we went to the Camino. There were about three people with learning disabilities and two members of staff. We walked ten miles a day. My personal experience, I didn't think I'd be able to do it because I'm partially sighted. I found it a bit difficult getting up and down hills but I achieved it. We did walks in the park for training. The first day I found it hard but we did it for quite a few days and it became quite easy.

Otto is a film star:

I'm doing a film. I actually started acting in school plays. Acting in front of people is actually quite exciting. I was in a new Jewish

---

* www.mylifemychoice.org.uk/pages/21-everyday-champions
† www.mylifemychoice.org
‡ I was appointed their first patron in 2018 after an intensive and lengthy selection process which included Thom Yorke and Alexander Armstrong. Probably one of my proudest moments.

film called *Samuel-613*. I played Joel. I was nominated for a BAFTA. Quite exciting things happen to me. I have been around the world. I went to been to India and Japan, Corfu, Los Angeles and Las Vegas. It was quite inspiring, mind-blowing adventure for me.

Two National Forums for families and learning-disabled people and local Partnership Boards were set up as an outcome of *Valuing People*.[37] These had some purchase and were lively and vocal. The funding was cut in 2017, however, to the deep disappointment of many involved. A report published in July 2019[38] identified 100 self-advocacy groups across England but these were unevenly spread with a lot of activity in the North-West and little in the East Midlands, South-West and London. This report suggested that self-advocates need to concentrate on earning money rather than just raising it, a nice place to meet is needed for people to get together, good volunteers can mean that groups can be run on little money, self-advocacy groups can learn a lot from each other, and self-advocacy helps people to get paid work. The report presents a bit of a mixed picture as questions were raised again about the definition of self-advocacy groups. Linking to the concern about representation, the report authors comment:

> We were disappointed that diversity – attracting people from Black and Minority Ethnic Groups, gay, Lesbian and bisexual, people with profound and multiple learning disabilities – was not a high priority.[39]

This raises the question of how great a role activism should play in the work of health and social care professionals. 'Whistleblowing', small acts of kindness, calling out poor practice, acting to shift things, bending the rules and sometimes breaking them. This is a tricky line and one I have struggled with in my own work. Bottom line for me is: if you are not prepared to act on injustices in whatever ways you can, it is probably time to think about a career change.

In terms of self-advocacy, we are left with patchy with pockets of brilliance, which is probably the most appropriate description for any area related to learning disability and/or autism in the UK.

> ## 2.12.2010
>
> Connor tells me you are after the top job at the Metropolitan Police. Apparently you would tell the protestors to calm down, go home and have a think about what they have done. We think the job should be yours!!

Chapter 7

Growing Older, Death and Dying

Previous chapters have outlined how many parents will have conducted considerable dependency work by the time they reach the age at which people typically retire. Carer's Allowance stops when people get their pensions, regardless of the work parents continue to do. A further and particularly grim poke in the eye for family carers. We know that paid employment may have been disrupted or impossible alongside caring responsibilities stretching across decades. This, again, has substantial economic and social implications for families. We also know that learning-disabled and/or autistic people will have had less opportunity to work and save money across their lives, are more likely to live in poor housing in deprived neighbourhoods, and are less likely to be married and have children, which increases the risk of isolation as people grow older.[1] It is also likely that older learning-disabled and/or autistic people will experience further layers of discrimination as ageing intersects with disability and other characteristics.

Family carers of older learning-disabled people report poorer physical health than their peers,[2] which can impact on the care they provide. Older learning-disabled people more commonly experience chronic health issues, such as kidney disease, dementia, constipation and diabetes, earlier than their non-disabled peers,[3] and recent research highlighted the over-use of antipsychotic medication, with 58% of those on antipsychotics reporting problem behaviours.[4] Finally, family life in older age has received little research attention, leaving us with patchy knowledge. Cos Michael, an autism and ageing consultant, in an editorial arguing why research is needed into the experiences of older autistic people, concludes:

> Researchers and funders expect high-quality support and care for their own families in their middle and later years and autistic people want the same. If we are to receive this support, it is obvious that research is necessary both to inform and equip those who provide it. To be blunt, because autistic people can be blunt – why do I even need to argue the case for research into autism and ageing?[5]

Planning for the future

So. Let's start by looking at what we do know. People are living longer in spite of the mortality rates identified by the CIPOLD review.[6] An increase of over a third in the number of learning-disabled people aged 60 and over was predicted between 2001 and 2021.[7] Dame Philippa Russell, former chair of the Standing Commission on Carers, reported in personal correspondence that her son's consultant recently referred to a 'new generation of survivors' who are now likely to outlive their parents. It is important to remember that even when people are supported to live in their own homes, family members can remain very much involved. Again, Mark Neary's blog is an insightful read here.[*]

Drawing on Chris Hatton's recent analysis of NHS Digital data,[†] an estimated 39% of learning-disabled people aged 65 or over are currently living in residential or nursing care. Hatton suggests these figures under-represent the actual figure because of the way in which the data is generated and because it is cheaper to fund generic rather than learning-disability-specific

---

[*]   https://markneary1dotcom1.wordpress.com
[†]   https://chrishatton.blogspot.com/2019/10

residential care (an average of £1033 per week compared with £626). (I know. The mind boggles on both counts.)

Projections for increases in life expectancy mean there will be a fourfold increase in the number of older learning-disabled people, with two-thirds living in the parental home. There is no available data about the number of older learning-disabled people in England, although Hatton[8] estimates that there are around 81,000 learning-disabled people aged over 50, many of whom are not in contact with services. Older parent caring is an increasing phenomenon and we know that thinking about the future is stressful for parents who may not be ready to make plans and/or who have concerns about the quality and appropriateness of available provision.[9] A review of six studies focusing on family carers[10] found fear for the future, lack of trust in services, lack of proactive support to manage crises and transitions, and declining personal support networks in a period when they are most needed. Another study found only 28% of participants had made plans for the future residential care of their children, and there was strong commitment to maintaining long-term home care for as long as possible.[11] The worry about the future, expressed by Jane and Amanda in Chapter 5, when their children were preschool, has a chilling tenacity.

It is well documented that the death of a family member, particularly the main caregiver, can trigger 'complicated' grieving and the need for crisis intervention for learning-disabled people.[12] Again, I suspect the complication is generated by the mishandling of end-of-life discussions with people, which I return to below. This is in part because parental loss is often accompanied by further losses, including the loss of home.[13] A recent pilot intervention aimed at supporting older carers to think about the future through social worker visits and the use of person-centred tools, in order to understand the needs of the family and develop future care plans, found that it was the first time most of the participants had been offered any support aimed at them.[14] Given the legal requirement to offer a carer's assessment, this is a further example of how policy is not translating into practice.

The lack of interest in older carers and lack of information about what to do clearly inhibits planning for the future.[15]

There is a National Institute for Health and Care Excellence (NICE) guideline 'Care and support of people growing older with learning disabilities',[16] which is full of sensible recommendations in this area. For example:

> Health and social care practitioners should work with the person and those most involved in their support to agree a plan for the future. Help them to make decisions before a crisis point or life-changing event is reached (for example, the death of a parent or a move to new housing).

These recommendations are simply recommendations, however, with no leverage behind them to ensure that they are enacted. NICE point to the need for studies of interventions to support families and people developing dementia, with existing UK studies showing a lack of preparedness of families.[17] Similarly, NICE identified a gap in evidence on applying advanced care planning in end-of-life care for learning-disabled people. This is despite UK studies showing how anxious families can be about this.[18] We know there is a substantial gap in knowledge here that is leaving families bereft of appropriate support.

And thinking about the here and now...

Everyday lives of older family carers and the daughters and sons they care for have been hit over the past decade with the cutting of service provision driven by the politics of austerity. Services such as day centres have been closed, alongside an increase in the eligibility criteria for those that remain.[19] This has obvious implications for families, reducing opportunities (albeit not necessarily shining opportunities) for people to go out, hang out with different people and do different activities. It also reduces the break that older carers get from their dependency work. Given that, by this stage, many of their peers will have retired and, if in good enough health, be enjoying spaces of rest and leisure, I assume this must pack quite a punch.

Recent research has highlighted how spaces of care are being weakened and diminished with these service cuts.[20] There is also some evidence of the agency and creativity people draw on to deal with changing levels of support. The potential 'care desert' is offset by patches of brilliance. These patches remain precarious, however, and have been summarized by Geoff DeVerteuil, reader in Urban and Social Geography, Cardiff University, as an 'assemblage of disparate hybridised and inherently precarious arrangements that exist side by side with residual arrangements from previous [care] settlements'.[21] A bit of a mouthful that can be summarized as overhang from the past mixed with cobbled-together bits of precarious care.

Love and caring in later life

I was involved in a project funded by Comic Relief called Embolden, led by Oxfordshire Family Support Network (OxFSN) in 2019. In Oxfordshire, 2940 carers of learning-disabled and/or autistic people aged 50 and over were identified. A key theme was concern about the future as illustrated in a short film produced as an earlier output of the project.[22] One father, 81, said, 'What keeps you awake at night is not knowing what the future holds for our son.' A mother, 92, said, 'I just dread that day. What is going to happen? If they decide to uproot her, I don't think she will survive.' Given that these children were babes and young tots around the time of the Ely Hospital scandal, this is not covering health and social care for learning-disabled and/or autistic people with much glory.

My role was to photograph a small group of older carers in their homes while they were interviewed by an OxFSN family advocate, Kathy Liddell. The people we met and the stories we heard were truly extraordinary and you can see a selection of the photos on the *Guardian* website* – carers in their 70s, 80s and 90s living with (or next door to, in one instance) their learning-disabled children who were in middle to late-middle age. In each of these homes, walls were covered in photos – weddings, holidays, school photos capturing happiness and love; there were knick-knacks and evidence of fun times, as well as the detritus of the labour of bureaucracy – lever arch files, paperwork piles and well-thumbed diaries.

In one beautifully neat living room in a small town, we sat on chairs and a settee that were facing a television and fireplace, with a window and large space behind them. In that space was a thick rug and a second, smaller television on a shelf with rows of DVDs. John, 81, described how his son, 49, went to the day centre two or three days a week; when he came home, he would sit on the rug in the living room watching DVDs on the smaller television. John and his wife have always had to juggle diaries to ensure someone was at home for Darryl. The biggest impact on their lives has been the lack of spontaneity as they are unable to leave Darryl on his own. There is grim irony that John was awarded an MBE for all the work he has done around learning disability and his wife was unable to attend the ceremony with him. John's love for Darryl was so clear throughout the interview. He still takes him swimming every Saturday at the club he set up. John hopes that Darryl will be able to move into supported living and lead a happy life. He worries he may be moved across the country to an unfamiliar place and with people he doesn't know. For John, he's not a family carer, 'it's just something you have been doing all your life...' He is just Dad.

Brenda was 92 and lived next door to her 62-year-old daughter, Karen. Brenda moved to Oxfordshire aged 17 to join the Land Army. She described how there was no schooling when she was younger – 'it was all about bombs and stuff'. She met her husband and they settled down to family life with four daughters. About 50 years ago, Brenda and her husband divorced, and her

* www.theguardian.com/society/gallery/2019/jun/11/family-carers-unsung-heroes-in-pictures

ex-husband died young. In retelling the story of her and Karen's lives, she wove a narrative of intense love, steely determination and a sense of peace and acceptance for her life. Her biggest fear, she said, was that after her death something would happen to her eldest daughter who had Karen to stay every weekend in a neighbouring village, and that Karen would be sent away to an institution. This fear is so intense that she described being unable to sleep at night; she would often get up, make a cup of tea in the early hours and doze off in a living-room chair.

There had been some rocky times for Karen and her mum over the years until Brenda found out about direct payments and started to organize her support. Her experiences with various health professionals were mixed, although she was very keen to thank those who have helped her. She recounted how, some years back when she was trying to arrange a Court of Protection order for her daughter, a social worker tried to block it saying that Karen was an adult and should be making her own choices about where to live and what to do. Brenda was devastated, but set about compiling a set of evidence to rebut each point raised. She was successful in the end.

Brenda finds the relentless paperwork she has to fill in very hard: 'Not a day goes by when one form or another has to be filled in – there is stacks and stacks of it!'

Another professional was due that Friday, and Brenda described how she had been asked to produce all of Karen's medical records and paperwork: 'I keep everything,' she said, 'I don't know where anything is when I need to find it, but I keep it all.' 'Where do you keep it all?' I asked, wondering at 62 years of documentation. 'Everywhere,' she replied, beaming, and I noticed notebooks and A4 pads stored vertically in between the armchairs and settee.

Every morning between 8 and 9am Brenda goes next door to see Karen, who has 24-hour care. She then waits at home for her daughter to go out for the day (to different local activities, the shops or to play football in the local park), and Brenda positions herself at her front door to welcome Karen home. 'It's so important to her,' said Brenda. 'I can see the look of joy on her face and relief that Mum is here. That is priceless to me.' Brenda's greatest wish would be to have another 20 years of life so she could continue to care for Karen.

Jo was in her early 80s and lives in a sheltered accommodation with her son, Ian, who is 50. Her younger son, Danny, 48, lives on the other side of the town in independent supported living, and since her husband died in 2006, Jo has been a single carer. Jo still struggles with guilt about the choices she has made for her two sons and whether she has done the right thing over the years. As I said earlier, the mother's toolkit contains a hefty wedge of guilt tucked away in it.

Ian phones daily and visits every Sunday for lunch and for anything else he needs, such as a cheque from his bank account. Jo has a range of support workers coming in to help with Danny, which include a family friend whom Danny loves dearly. Jo can't go out without Danny even though he is OK to be left for a short time. If she goes out and he gets anxious, he phones 999 on the landline. Reflecting on her life as a carer, Jo said emphatically that she wouldn't change it: 'It is equally frustrating and rewarding,' she said, 'and it's all about love at the end of the day.' Jo had been told she could leave Danny at the hospital when he was born with Down's syndrome. Fifty years later, the horror she felt at this suggestion remains palpable.

Jo's advice to other carers is to 'expect the unexpected and embrace whatever happens as it is not what happens to you but how you deal with it that is important'. Like Brenda, Jo's biggest fear is what will happen to her sons when she is no longer around. She hopes they will always have someone to love and care for them, that someone will always give Ian a big hug and that he will be able to continue living in the flat he shares with her.

Mary and Peter, who are in their 80s, live with their 53-year-old daughter, Judy. (Names have been changed.) The day centre Judy attends has recently been merged with a day centre for elderly people because of cuts. Like John, the couple reflect on the way in which their time is structured and inflexible. Their caring day starts at 7am, when they get Judy ready to go out, and ends at 10pm, when she goes to bed. They have to be at home at 2.45pm during the week to wait for the bus bringing Judy home. The bus could arrive anytime between 3 and 4.15pm, depending on traffic.

This brought back memories for me. The tyranny of the school transport. For 15 years either Rich or I had to be home to meet Connor off the school bus, which had a similar time-of-arrival window to Judy's bus. There was no asking another parent to pick your child up from school if you got held up in a meeting. And no gradual move towards coming home from school independently with the proud ownership of a door key. The bus had to be met. My brain juddered a bit listening to the couple talk about this detail with such expression and feeling. Over 50 years spent waiting for their daughter to come home on a bus. In contrast, at the weekends, the couple go out with Judy, shopping on a Saturday and an outing on Sunday to a garden centre, a drive or out for lunch. Mary and Peter think it's hard for friends and neighbours to understand what their lives are like. Judy brings a lot of love, joy and laughter to their lives, but the couple worry about her health and her future.

Jean's son, Kevin, 50, lives in supported living outside of Oxfordshire and they take it in turns to visit each other every weekend. It is a three-hour round trip by public transport, but nothing stops Jean making that journey. Like the other parents, the worst thing for Jean is the 'worry and uncertainty when you are no longer around' and how Kevin will cope when she is no longer there. With Kevin out of county, Jean's daughter has said she will not be able to see him every weekend as Jean does now and that it would be easier if Kevin lived nearer. Jean says, 'Am I ever going to get him back into the county? I just don't know.'

Common themes across these different stories are: parents do not see themselves as 'family carers'; considerations (and sometimes concern) about the future role their other children will play in the care; the intensity of their support (and protection) of

145

their daughter or son; a wish to live into much older age in order to continue this. They all seemed incredibly youthful, energetic and spirited, although one couple, Mary and Peter, were a bit put out when one of their other children said that their daughter Judy was keeping them young. Again, the lack of recognition or understanding of the dependency work these parents had undertaken for decades is striking.

Gaining a brief insight into the lives of older carers was powerful and moving. 'Well, you don't retire, of course,' said one person. I was struck by the stoicism, lack of moaning or whinging, and the energy. Several people said, 'You just have to get on with it, as simple as that.' The typical aches, pains and twinges of older age seem to be subsumed into focus on the task ahead, making sure their children's later lives were as sorted as they could possibly be, despite the uncertainties generated by the ever-present threat of cuts to services and a continual stream of atrocity stories dripping across local and national media.

Thinking about autism

There will be different trajectories here for autistic people without learning disabilities as many people work and have successful careers, relationships and families. In the Healthtalk project, two of the participants were aged over 60. John, 63, was diagnosed with Asperger syndrome two years before the interview, after a discussion about autism with fellow members of a psychotherapy group encouraged him to go to his GP. John was diagnosed by a clinical psychologist and described feeling a sense of relief because somebody finally understood what he was like. John's story was moving and poignant, and I went on to write about his narrative.[23] It was a story of loss, 'mishaps' and misunderstandings because his autism diagnosis came so late in his life:

> And somebody younger, if that was assessed. If somebody younger was seen and assessed, screened and somebody would say well

look don't do anything drastic, we will help you to make the most of it, to make the most of your life. And you will live a profitable and productive life and we are not going to mollycoddle you, but we will be there to keep an eye on you from afar as it were, you know, to make sure you are not going to get yourself into serious difficulties and my life would have been completely different.

He was a brilliant raconteur, and his story was dense with recollections and memories of different experiences, particularly about employment.

John was brought up by his grandmother after his mother entered a psychiatric hospital when he was a baby. He had a good childhood and describes not getting on badly at school but not getting on particularly well. He was excellent at French and English but 'pretty useless at everything else'. His father told him that in order to succeed in life you had to be good at maths, and John took this literally. He did not like football or any form of conflict or contact, and avoided being bullied at school by keeping his head down.

John describes having a long history of misreading people and this, combined with his strong work ethic, has led to him having a series of jobs over the years in which he has been taken for granted, exploited or abused. He has a strong eye for detail, is efficient and competent within the workplace, but cannot multi-task. He has suffered from depression and no longer works. He went back to college to study languages and did very well, but could not complete the courses.

Now John lives on his own and finds it difficult to keep his house organized. His house is cluttered with books, magazines, newspapers and 'mountains of stuff'. A support worker visits him every two or three weeks and helps him to sort out things, but he would like more support with his domestic life. He meets up with a group of autistic people in a local pub each week, which he enjoys, and he gets on very well with people. John feels that he has spent his life being good at French and trying hard, but that he has somehow missed out: 'It is as if I am walking around and everybody has got it but me because I have got Asperger's.'

What is particularly relevant here was the lack of appropriate support John received from social care. He was very clear that he didn't want people coming round to do his cleaning or sorting out his house for him; he wanted someone to tell or remind him to do it himself. He found it too easy to lose himself in French newspapers and ignore life around him. I asked him what he did each day:

Waste time. I feel that I am wasting time. Make things to do really. I make things to do. There is no structure in my life. There is no structure. I don't have to do anything, you know. It is not laziness, I mean people could think it is laziness but it is to do with... I walk around in a sort of state of muddle, muddlement, you know, I am very often muddled... It sort of paralyses you. I don't know if there is a better way to put it...it is a lack of clarity, lack of clarity of thought. It is like a lack of perspicacity in my thought even...

You know I manage to fill my days. I fill my days in bloody Tesco's and wandering around and reading bits and not reading anything properly in depth but just reading bits of this and bits of that you know. As I said, I have got the French and German newspapers and that. But it is all bits here and bits there. It is not, there is nothing constructive about it. Nothing structured about it. Nothing, you know, it is just filling in time.

Peter had led a very successful working life as a scientist. Married with one son, he was diagnosed aged 80, and I spoke with him and his wife when he was 83. Peter realized he was autistic after reading a book that described his lack of empathy and lack of engagement with his surroundings. Peter has been counselled for the past three years and has become more aware of some of the extremes of his behaviour, such as intolerance, and how to control his temper. Peter described being always focused on things that interest him, and that he is, by nature, a loner. He has had an obsession with time since childhood and is often very rude to people without thinking about it. He enjoyed a fascinating childhood in Vienna, from which developed a lifelong love of music and the arts. His wife, a former actress, describes having made significant compromises in her life to adapt to Peter's ways; she often felt lonely during their marriage. She has found Peter's retirement particularly difficult, and both Peter and his wife have suffered from stress and depression:

> I am perfectly content, put it that way, to sit and read what interests me and forget there is anybody around. My wife says I sit there and I might as well be in a library where nobody is allowed to talk because I can sit and not say anything. Or that she will say something and it will just, you know bounce off, I won't react to it. Or I think when we are talking that whatever she had to say she has finished and I will walk out not realizing that there is a lot more that should be said. I am beginning to realize that but throughout my life up to now I hadn't really thought of that. I've just felt, well I want to go and do this, so what. And I have had very little patience with say, people who haven't had to...as my wife says I have been extremely lucky in my vocation and able to absorb things easily, who haven't got my knowledge or experience and education and I sort of feel well why should I bother with you?

While Peter and his wife clearly loved each other, their story was one of substantial difficulties and challenges experienced by the non-autistic partner. Like John, this is, in part, because of the lack of diagnosis which can both enable people to recognize bits of their behaviour that are problematic in a relationship and enable partners to better understand some of that behaviour. Another participant described her relief at her husband's autism diagnosis in his 50s because it meant she was living with an autistic partner rather than 'a deeply selfish one'. Peter was indignant that his request for a diagnosis from a renowned diagnostic centre was rejected because of his age; it is clear that the knowledge that he was autistic helped him to better understand some of his actions and he was determined to try to change that.

Grief and bereavement

Trawling through the literature in preparation for writing this section was another grim experience. I narrowed the search to articles since 2016 to try to get past the pathological work, but it just keeps coming. Searching for 'grief' and 'autism' turned up work focusing on the grief mothers experience when their children are diagnosed with autism. A very recent study called it 'an actual death'.[24] Switching the search to learning disability was not a lot better as there is a focus on whether or not people actually understand what death means. There is some sensible work highlighting how learning-disabled people have been excluded from end-of-life discussions because 'ignorance is bliss' and people won't understand, or because of not wanting to burden people.[25] These assumptions seem to continue unabated across people's lifetimes. Unsurprisingly, there is evidence that involvement in bereavement rituals can be beneficial and a strong argument that learning-disabled people 'experience bereavement and grief in a manner similar to that of the general population', suggesting 'the need for open communication, facilitation of informed choice, and a culture of inclusion'.[26]

Support workers can find negotiating death with people difficult because of a lack of confidence and feelings of anxiety about it. There is a circular failing here as 'death secrecy' can lead to people not being able to understand why someone is no longer around.[27] Staff training is essential, along with support for staff, appropriate resources such as the Beyond Words book *When Somebody Dies*[28] and the development of formal policies and procedures.

End-of-life care

I mentioned earlier the mortality rates of autistic patients which found that autistic people are likely to die earlier than the mainstream population across each death category. Learning-disabled people are more likely to die from pneumonia, aspiration pneumonitis, epilepsy and complications of Down's syndrome.[29] We know that learning-disabled people face significant inequalities in end-of-life care,[30] which is no big surprise given the inequalities experienced across their lifetime. This is because of failings in healthcare delivery, poor communication and inaccessible information, co-morbidities (having more than one health condition) and a dependency on people such as carers to recognize health problems.[31] Recommendations to improve the health and social care people receive centre on annual health checks and the provision of reasonable adjustments, although it is not clear that a dent has been made into the failings here.[32] Anecdotal evidence shows that good-quality care is likely to be the outcome of committed professionals rather than the organizational culture of the Trust.[33]

There is very little research focusing on the end-of-life care for learning-disabled and/or autistic people,[34] and what is known is a cacophony, almost, of failings across the board. We seem to find it difficult to identify end of life in learning-disabled and/or autistic patients,[35] which I find a bit baffling. There can be difficulties in communication which can impact on identifying pain and assessing treatment, challenges in involvement in end-of-life decision making, lack of experienced health and social care professionals, and lack of support staff knowledge about supporting people at the end of life.[36]

Of course, discrepant views can exist between learning-disabled people, their families and practitioners on the subject of end-of-life care and 'bad news' decisions.[37] A study of the experiences of older learning-disabled people in hospitals showed poor care experiences due to the inability of staff to communicate effectively, and carers felt behaviours that challenge were likely to precipitate inappropriate early discharge.[38] Studies of carer experience of palliative care, cancer and dementia[39] found concerns about how to access palliative care services and how to communicate the prognosis and treatments required to families and to older learning-disabled people with deteriorating health. Social care staff in palliative care settings with people with Down's syndrome and dementia experienced dissonance between their enabling role supporting autonomy and their subsequent role of monitoring deteriorating health and diminishing skills.[40]

Essentially, people are subjected to the failings they typically receive across their life course, only the end point is obviously so final. People die of a dire range of conditions that have been largely eradicated for the mainstream population. Richard Handley,* for example, died in 2012 of constipation when he was 33. His devastated family showed the coroner photographs of the size of Richard's stomach in the days before he died, likening it to a full-term pregnancy, and yet this was not investigated by health professionals.

In 2016, Joe Ulleri died a preventable death after being left without food for 19 days in hospital after suffering from an unexplained fall at home.[41] His inquest was also live-tweeted by George Julian.† The unfolding story of harrowing neglect by the hospital involved was countered by the description of members of the L'Arche community he lived in, who maintained a 24-hour watch by his bedside while he was in hospital using a WhatsApp group as an organizational tool. It was very clear that this was a close and loving family.

On 10 March 2017, a 38-year-old woman, Jo-Jo, died of scabies in Hackney having been diagnosed with 'probable crushed scabies' in 2013.[42] The safeguarding review is a grim read, outlining how poorly Jo-Jo was let down by the various agencies who should have been supporting her. This included Hackney Council, her GP practice, the district nurse team, Homerton and Royal London NHS Trust and Goldsmith Personnel which provided community outreach workers. No consideration had been made of Jo-Jo's mother's capacity to look after her daughter's skin condition. Ian Winter, the author of the review stated: 'It is difficult not to conclude that her learning disability played a part in these gaps and omissions, and so too perhaps the assumed social standing of her mother.'[43] Amanda Elliot of Healthwatch Hackney, said:

---

* See https://twitter.com/HandleyInquest for more information about Richard's inquest.
† https://twitter.com/JoeInquest

There's something deeply wrong when a woman with a learning disability is dying from complications from a skin condition in the 21st century. As a society it's unacceptable. It's an othering that takes place. People don't actually see people with learning disabilities as having human rights.[44]

Where does this leave us?

I feel an intense sadness that lifetimes can be spent trying to create a safe life for family members. As a society, we simply do not care enough. Waiting for a bus at 3pm for 50 or more years, dreading further cuts to already patchy services and wanting to stay alive long enough to protect adult offspring are an appalling indictment of the organization and delivery of health and social care. Human rights seem to stop at the front door when people are learning disabled and/or autistic.

What can you do?

- Remember that parents and older carers have probably had a bellyful over the years in a range of different shapes, sizes and flavours.

- Try to imagine living in fear of the future; listen to the stories and keep the human at the forefront of your practice.

- Work with families early on to develop trust and start the conversation about future plans with sensitivity and care.

- Keep those professional lenses clear to see beyond the label to any health ailments.

- Remember that learning disability is not a cause of death.

The dentist

POSTED 29 MAY 2012

'LB saw the dentist at school today...'

'Wow! Did you, LB?'

'Yes, Mum.'

'What did they say?'

'Open your mouth, Mum.'

Chapter 8

The Outlook: Patchy with Pockets of Brilliance

TIME FOR CHANGE

Crumbs, I was aiming for the moon, the stars and more in writing this book... Such big claims back in Chapter 1:

> To generate a space free from jargon and empty concepts, from the constraints and weight of 'official' processes and discourses – a space in which the love, laughter and joy that is woven through families such as ours can shine through, alongside the challenges.

At times, I ended up feeling like a cartoon character pounding along a running track, deflecting flying boulders with wacky wristbands. And the boulders just kept coming: the drag that keeps dragging us back centuries.

Fears articulated when children were tots materialized decades later against a backdrop of a 'scandal, review and repeat' cycle. Scandals that, ironically, can improve overall services and support while leaving the people at the centre of the scandal untouched. I mentioned in Chapter 2 how the Ely Hospital inquiry led to the setting up of the precursor of the CQC. The Mazars review, commissioned on the back of Connor's death, led to an NHS England 'Learning from Deaths' [1]programme in which the focus on learning disability became pretty much all but invisible.

I have no idea what impact, if any, this programme has had, but conversations at the time were around raising the bar more broadly across the NHS in terms of preventable deaths, rather than a focus on one group. The rationale was that this would benefit everyone.

This is the stumbling point. Improvements for everyone do not include everyone. This is the inclusion phobia. Everyone is a mainstream everyone – people already in privileged positions. Those on the margins remain untouched.

Eva Kittay, who has kind of sat on my shoulder as I thought about and wrote this book, says:

> As those who plow the fields of social justice know, an oppression that has laid so heavy on the shoulders of its victims that it has numbed the response to the burden is the most unjust of all.[2]

Oppressions have laid so heavy, and in so many ways responses to this have been numbed. The playing out of atrocities in full view with little or no effective action. The 'insane' actions we saw in Chapters 1, 4 and 6. Evidence of numbing. Of accepting the truly unacceptable.

I return here to Nigel Evans's commentary on Terry Green's attempt to turn the wheels of his wheelchair in Borocourt:

> For decades the full panoply of the medical profession has trooped through this ward and no one had the wit, the initiative or imagination to give Terry this opportunity.[*]

The wit, initiative and imagination... We aren't asking for the moon on a stick, and yet an enduring, collective ignorance remains. A refusal, wilful or otherwise, to get Terry Green the means of a measure of independence after spending 40 years in bed and ten on a beanbag. An acceptance of standards we would never condone for most others. A home, down a dark lane, with a high fence and 'no smoking' signs on the wall.

At the same time, love remains undiminished. It is like a fierce fire in our hearts and that love, that intense and beautiful love, generates determination and action in families. Determination

---

[*]   *The Silent Minority*. Accessed on 10/2/2020 at www.youtube.com/watch?v=7Qb424HvKSQ

to generate spaces of acceptance. To demonstrate the worth and value of our children. Over and over again. In 2019 Katherine Runswick-Cole and I updated our liminal paper from 2008.[3] We sought to unpack why there had been such limited success around campaigns for disabled children, and suggested maternal activism has become stuck in a cycle of failure because of the constant fracturing of the movement. A commitment to naive optimism by some and bitter cynicism by others.

We argued that alternatives to traditional understandings of maternal activism are necessary and used #JusticeforLB as an example of collective activism. This social movement gathered and generated brilliance, colour and joy in an unprecedented way. Our overall conclusion in the paper was to argue for a shift in the responsibility for activism away from mothers to a community response to social injustice. Indeed, in Chapter 4 I underlined the importance of prioritizing a social justice framework in tackling systemic rigidities.

There is nothing to stop professionals being part of a community response to injustice.

If we were all to weave this strand through our everyday actions and activities, be they in or outside of paid work, things can only get better. Responding to injustice is only a small step away from behaving with decency, respect and thoughtfulness.

The sparkling tweets dotted across this book provide examples of this, and there were so many I have not been able to include.

Pug memes in appointment letters, enabling the touching of clocks in a GP surgery, being prepared to meet children in whatever way works, including on the stairs, on the floor or pretty much under a household pet. Some of this stuff is truly extraordinary, some basic humanity:

> Incredible paramedics carrying Joey in full status epilepticus
> down three stories from my top floor flat into the ambulance,

while chattering to Bea (5) about Harry Potter, and keeping me calm. (Steve Unwin – @RoseUnwin)

Our new GP after having everything swept off his desk & kicked in my son's meltdown, very gently asking me if I was ok & phoning later to see what he could do to help. (Helen MC – @SherlockHMC)

Paramedics consistently shine in our experiences and in many shared stories. I wonder if the 'emergency' framing and focus punts other trumped-up considerations off the nearest bridge. There's an immediacy of intimate human interaction that kicks in. One final example involves a nurse who seems to have got her 'wise' stripes sorted:

I'll never forget the nurse I was way too blunt with on a ward when our care was going wrong. You'd hear nurses put themselves forward for certain patients each morn – thought she'd avoid me at all costs. Next day, there was her name in marker pen on the board next to my sons. She'd recognized I was just exhausted & scared. It was early days & we were just realizing his condition. She spent the next few weeks with us – working with me as a team & getting us a plan. She could have just avoided me & not picked the tricky case. I'll never forget that. (Sarah Ricketts – @ SarahR_123)

The families who took part in the Healthtalk project were asked if they had any messages for professionals, and this generated some interesting and overlapping points which I've grouped into three sections.

Listening and reflection

Listen to families and think about what they are telling you. Take guidance from them. Understand the stresses and strains families may be under. Don't atomize the child or children; think about the family. Stresses, strains and challenges can fluctuate over time. Be proactive: don't let the families always do the running. Check if advice has worked and be prepared.

Don't assume that families that seem to be coping at one point will remain buoyant. Don't let the label or diagnosis blinker you; dig deeper for reasons why someone may seem under the weather or less happy. Leave the window of possibilities, aspirations and imagination well and truly open and always see the human.

Communication

Be respectful and welcoming to parents. Avoid jargon, acronyms and complicated words/explanations. Be honest and say when you do not have an answer or knowledge about autism or learning disabilities. Ensure coherent advice and guidance is provided across all professionals. Follow through on actions and keep families informed.

Information

Make sure families are signposted to the right person if you cannot deal with that particular issue. Embed advice and guidance given in the context of that family. Families don't know what they don't know (and sometimes don't know what they do know!). Try not to assume they have relevant information at the appropriate time.

None of the above cost much in terms of money or time. Just a good dose of understanding, sensitivity and thoughtfulness. A willingness to bend the rules to get the job done, every so often, and a recognition of people as humans.

This is what it boils down to at the end of the day. It really is this simple. We are all human.

Endnotes

Preface

1   Ryan, S. (2018) *Justice for Laughing Boy: Connor Sparrowhawk – A Death by Indifference*. London: Jessica Kingsley Publishers.

2   Hatton, C., Glover, G., Emerson, E. and Brown, I. (2016) *Learning Disabilities Observatory. People with Learning Disabilities in England 2015: Main Report*. London: Public Health England.

3   The Learning Disability Mortality Review (LeDeR) Programme (2018) *Annual Report 2018*. Accessed on 2/12/2020 at www.bristol.ac.uk/media-library/sites/sps/leder/LeDeR_Annual_Report_2018%20published%20May%202019.pdf

4   Bates, K., Goodley, D. and Runswick-Cole, K. (2017) 'Precarious lives and resistant possibilities: The labour of people with learning disabilities in times of austerity.' *Disability and Society 32*, 2, 160–175.

5   McVilly, K.R., Stancliffe, R.J., Parmenter, T.R. and Burton-Smith, R.M. (2006) '"I get by with a little help from my friends": Adults with intellectual disability discuss loneliness.' *Journal of Applied Research in Intellectual Disabilities 19*, 2, 191–203.

6   Abbott, D. and Burns, J. (2007) 'What's love got to do with it? Experiences of lesbian, gay, and bisexual people with intellectual disabilities in the United Kingdom and views of the staff who support them.' *Sexuality Research and Social Policy 4*, 1, 27–39.

7   Reinders, J.S. (2002) 'The good life for citizens with intellectual disability.' *Journal of Intellectual Disability Research 46*, 1, 1–5.

8   Featherstone, H. (1980) *A Difference in the Family: Life with a Disabled Child*. New York, NY: Basic Books.

9   Goodley, D. (2014) *Dis/ability Studies: Theorising Disablism and Ableism*. Abingdon: Routledge.

10 Hevey, D. (1992) *The Creatures Time Forgot: Photography and Disability Imagery*. London: Routledge, p.51.

Chapter 1

1   Goodey, C.F. (2015) *Learning Disability and Inclusion Phobia: Past, Present, Future*. Abingdon: Routledge, p.9.

2   Goffman, E. (1963) *Stigma: Notes on the Management of Spoiled Identity*. Englewood Cliffs, NJ: Prentice-Hall.

3   Goffman [**PQ**](n xxx), p.41.

4   Pavlopoulou, G. and Dimitriou, D. (2019) '"I don't live with autism; I live with my sister". Sisters' accounts on growing up with their preverbal autistic siblings.' *Research in Developmental Disabilities 88*, 1–15.

5   Hewitson, J. (2018) *Autism: How to Raise a Happy Autistic Child*. London: Orion.
6   Cook, B. and Garnett, M. (eds) (2018) *Spectrum Women*. London: Jessica Kingsley Publishers.
7   James, L. (2017) *Odd Girl Out: An Autistic Woman in a Neurotypical World*. London: Bluebird.
8   Kim, C. (2014) *Nerdy, Shy, and Socially Inappropriate: A User Guide to an Asperger Life*. London: Jessica Kingsley Publishers.
9   Silverman, C. (2012) *Understanding Autism*. Princeton, NJ: Princeton University Press.

Chapter 2

1   Digby, A. and Wright, D. (eds) (2002) *From Idiocy to Mental Deficiency: Historical Perspectives on People with Learning Disabilities*. Abingdon: Routledge.
2   Silberman, S. (2015) *Neurotribes: The Legacy of Autism and How to Think Smarter About People Who Think Differently*. Crows Nest: Allen & Unwin.
3   McFadden, J. (2007) 'A shameful history.' *The Guardian*. Accessed on 10/2/2020 at www.theguardian.com/commentisfree/2007/oct/22/comment.genetics
4   Raw, L. (2018) 'Support for eugenics never really went away, but this is how it's becoming mainstream again.' *The Independent*. Accessed on 10/2/2020 at www.independent.co.uk/voices/eugenics-ucl-toby-young-conference-how-it-became-mainstream-a8154316.html
5   People's Collection Wales (2017) 'Ely Hospital: Mark Drakeford on the Ely report whistleblower.' Accessed on 10/2/2020 at www.peoplescollection.wales/items/582312
6   Morris, P. (1969) *Put Away: Institutions for the Mentally Retarded*. New York, NY: Atherton Press.
7   Morris (n xxx), p.xxiv.
8   The King's Fund (1982) 'An ordinary life: Comprehensive locally based residential services for mentally handicapped people.' Accessed on 23/2/2010 at https://archive.kingsfund.org.uk/concern/published_works/000001408?locale=pt-BR#?c=0&m=0&s=0&cv=0&xywh=-2265%2C-4%2C5974%2C1872
9   Department of Health (1989) *Caring for People: Community Care in the Next Decade and Beyond*, Cm 849. London: HMSO.
10 Department of Health and Social Care (2001) *Valuing People: A New Strategy for Learning Disability for the 21st Century*. Accessed on 23/2/2020 at www.gov.uk/government/publications/valuing-people-a-new-strategy-for-learning-disability-for-the-21st-century
11 Mencap (2007) *Death by Indifference: Following up the* Treat Me Right! *Report*. Accessed on 23/2/2020 at www.mencap.org.uk/sites/default/files/2016-06/DBIreport.pdf
12 Michael, J. (2008) *Healthcare for All: Report of the Independent Inquiry into Access to Healthcare for People with Learning Disabilities*. Accessed on 13/2/2020 at https://webarchive.nationalarchives.gov.uk/20130105064250/http://www.dh.gov.uk/en/Publicationsandstatistics/Publications/PublicationsPolicyAndGuidance/DH_099255
13 Department of Health (2010) *Valuing People Now: Summary Report March 2009–September 2010*. Accessed on 23/2/2020 at https://assets.publishing.service.gov.uk/government/uploads/system/uploads/attachment_data/file/215891/dh_122387.pdf
14 Heslop, P., Blair, P., Fleming, P., Hoghton, M., Marriott, A. and Russ, L. (2013) *Confidential Inquiry into Premature Deaths of People with Learning Disabilities*. Accessed on 12/2/202 at www.bristol.ac.uk/media-library/sites/cipold/migrated/documents/fullfinalreport.pdf

15 https://www.theguardian.com/society/2013/jul/12/no-review-board-deaths-learning-difficulties

16 Norah Fry Centre for Disability Studies (2017) 'Learning Disabilities Mortality Review (LeDeR).' Accessed on 10/2/2020 at www.bristol.ac.uk/sps/leder

17 Hirvikoski, T., Mittendorfer-Rutz, E., Boman, M., Larsson, H., Lichtenstein, P. and Bölte, S. (2016) 'Premature mortality in autism spectrum disorder.' *British Journal of Psychiatry 208*, 3, 232–238.

18 Connolly, K. (2018) 'Hans Asperger aided and supported Nazi programme, study says.' *The Guardian*. Accessed on 23/2/2020 at www.theguardian.com/world/2018/apr/19/hans-asperger-aided-and-supported-nazi-programme-study-says

19 Kanner, L. (1943) 'Autistic disturbances of affective contact.' *Nervous Child 2*, 3, 217–250.

20 Kanner, L. (1944) 'Early infantile autism.' *Journal of Pediatrics 25*, 3, 211–217.

21 Lehmann-Haupt, C. (1997) 'An icon of psychology falls from his pedestal.' *The New York Times*. Accessed on 23/2/2020 at www.nytimes.com/1997/01/13/books/an-icon-of-psychology-falls-from-his-pedestal.html

22 Bettelheim, B. (1967) *The Empty Fortress: Infantile Autism and the Birth of the Self*. New York, NY: The Free Press.

23 Wing, L. (1981) 'Asperger's syndrome: A clinical account.' *Psychological Medicine 11*, 1, 115–129.

24 Milton, D.E. (2012) 'On the ontological status of autism: The "double empathy problem".' *Disability and Society 27*, 6, 883–887.

25 Department of Health and Social Care (2011) 'Fulfilling and rewarding lives: The strategy for adults with autism in England.' Accessed on 23/2/2020 at www.gov.uk/government/news/fulfilling-and-rewarding-lives-the-strategy-for-adults-with-autism-in-england

26 Department of Health and Social Care, Department for Business, Innovation and Skills, Department for Education, Department for Transport, Department for Work and Pensions, Ministry of Justice (2014) *'Think Autism': An update to the government adult autism strategy*. Accessed on 23/2/2020 at www.gov.uk/government/publications/think-autism-an-update-to-the-government-adult-autism-strategy

27 The Westminster Commission on Autism (2016) *A Spectrum of Obstacles: An Inquiry into Access to Healthcare for Autistic People*. Accessed on 14/2/2020 at https://westminsterautismcommission.files.wordpress.com/2016/03/ar1011_ncg-autism-report-july-2016.pdf

28 Local Government Association, Directors of Adult Social Services, NHS England (2017) *Transforming Care. Model Service Specifications*. Accessed on 23/2/2020 at www.england.nhs.uk/wp-content/uploads/2017/02/model-service-spec-2017.pdf

29 Lomas, C. (2020) 'Ten people with learning disabilities or autism died in secure hospitals in past year.' Sky News, 14 January. Accessed on 10/2/2020 at https://news.sky.com/story/ten-people-with-learning-disabilities-or-autism-died-in-secure-hospitals-in-past-year-11902258

30 Clements, L. and Read, J. (2008) 'Life, Disability and the Pursuit of Human Rights.' In L. Clements and J. Read (eds) *Disabled People and the Right to Life: The Protection and Violation of Disabled People's Most Basic Human Rights*. Abingdon: Routledge, p.6.

31 Booth, R. (2018) 'One in five Britons with disabilities have their rights violated, UN told.' *The Guardian*. Accessed on 23/2/2020 at www.theguardian.com/society/2018/oct/07/one-in-five-britons-with-disabilities-have-their-rights-violated-un-told

32 Pring, J. (2020) 'Government faces legal action over failure to stop ATU "atrocities".' Disability News Service. Accessed on 23/2/2020 at www.disabilitynewsservice.com/government-faces-legal-action-over-failure-to-stop-atu-atrocities

33 Mencap (2003) 'Breaking Point: A report on caring without a break for children and adults with severe or profound learning disabilities.' Accessed on 10/2/2020 at www.mencap.org.uk/sites/default/files/2016-07/campaigns_breaking_point_0408.pdf

Chapter 3

1 Crane, L., Chester, J.W., Goddard, L., Henry, L.A. and Hill, E. (2016) 'Experiences of autism diagnosis: A survey of over 1000 parents in the United Kingdom.' *Autism 20*, 2, 153–162; Boshoff, K., Gibbs, D., Phillips, R.L., Wiles, L. and Porter, L. (2018) 'A meta-synthesis of how parents of children with autism describe their experience of advocating for their children during the process of diagnosis.' *Health and Social Care in the Community 27*, 4, e143–e157.
2 Crane *et al.* (n xxx).
3 Crane *et al.* (n xxx); Boshoff, K., Gibbs, D., Phillips, R.L., Wiles, L. and Porter, L. (2018) 'A meta-synthesis of how parents of children with autism describe their experience of advocating for their children during the process of diagnosis.' *Health and Social Care in the Community 27*, 4, e143–e157.
4 Ryan, S. and Salisbury, H. (2012) '"You know what boys are like": Pre-diagnosis experiences of parents of children with autism spectrum conditions.' *British Journal of General Practice 62*, 598, e378–e38.
5 Crane *et al.* (n xxx), p.160.
6 Ryan and Salisbury (n xxx).

Chapter 4

1 Avery, D. (1997) 'RE: age onset of disability, Message to Disability-Research discussion group, 9th June.'
2 Kittay, E. (1999) *Love's Labour: Essays on Women, Equality, and Dependency.* New York, NY: Routledge.
3 Hatton, C., Emerson, E., Graham, H., Blacher, J. and Llewellyn, G. (2010) 'Changes in family composition and marital status in families with a young child with cognitive delay.' *Journal of Applied Research in Intellectual Disabilities 23*, 1, 14–26.
4 Blackburn, C., Spencer, N. and Read, J. (2010) 'Prevalence of childhood disability and the characteristics and circumstances of disabled children in the UK: Secondary analysis of the Family Resources Survey.' *BMC Pediatrics 10*, 21.
5 Clements, L. and Broach, S. (eds) (2020) *Disabled Children and the Law.* London: Legal Action Group.
6 Clements and Broach (n xxx), p.21.
7 Kittay (n xxx), p.169.
8 City and Hackney Safeguarding Adults Board (2019) 'Safeguarding Adult Review into Death of JoJo.' Accessed on 11/2/2020 at http://files.localgov.co.uk/jojo-sar.pdf
9 Rapp, R. (2004) *Testing Women, Testing the Fetus: The Social Impact of Amniocentesis in America.* New York, NY: Routledge.
10 Silverman, C. (2012) *Understanding Autism.* Princeton, NJ: Princeton University Press.
11 Milton, D. (2018) 'A critique of the use of Applied Behavioural Analysis (ABA): On behalf of the Neurodiversity Manifesto Steering Group.' Accessed on 13/2/2020 at https://kar.kent.ac.uk/69268/1/Applied%20behaviour%20analysis.pdf
12 Mitchell, W. and Sloper, P. (2000) *User-Friendly Information for Families with Disabled Children: A Guide to Good Practice.* York: Joseph Rowntree Foundation.
13 Clements, L. and Read, J. (2008) 'Life, Disability and the Pursuit of Human Rights.' In L. Clements and J. Read (eds) *Disabled People and the Right to Life: The Protection and Violation of Disabled People's Most Basic Human Rights.* Abingdon: Routledge.
14 Hatton, C., Akram, Y., Shah, R., Robertson, J. and Emerson, E. (2004) *Supporting South Asian Families with a Child with Severe Disabilities.* London: Jessica Kingsley Publishers.

15 Ali, Z., Fazil, Q., Bywaters, P., Wallace, L. and Singh, G. (2001) 'Disability, ethnicity and childhood: A critical review of research.' *Disability and Society 16*, 7, 949–967.

16 Liasidou, A. (2012) 'Inclusive education and critical pedagogy at the intersections of disability, race, gender and class.' *Journal for Critical Education Policy Studies 10*, 1, 168–184.

17 Fox, F., Aabe, N., Turner, K., Redwood, S. and Rai, D. (2017) '"It was like walking without knowing where I was going": A qualitative study of autism in a UK Somali migrant community.' *Journal of Autism and Developmental Disorders 47*, 2, 305–315.

18 Fox, F., Aabe, N., Turner, K., Redwood, S. and Rai, D. (2017) '"It was like walking without knowing where I was going": A qualitative study of autism in a UK Somali migrant community.' *Journal of Autism and Developmental Disorders 47*, 2, p. 308.

19 Munroe, K., Hammond, L. and Cole, S. (2016) 'The experiences of African immigrant mothers living in the United Kingdom with a child diagnosed with an autism spectrum disorder: An interpretive phenomenological analysis.' *Disability and Society 31*, 6, 798–819.

20 Ferraioli, S.J. and Harris, S.L. (2009) 'The impact of autism on siblings.' *Social Work in Mental Health 8*, 1, 41–53.

21 Lovell, B. and Wetherell, M.A. (2016) 'The psychophysiological impact of childhood autism spectrum disorder on siblings.' *Research in Developmental Disabilities 49*, 226–234.

22 Connors, C. and Stalker, K. (2002) *The Views and Experiences of Disabled Children and Their Siblings: A Positive Outlook*. London: Jessica Kingsley Publishers.

23 Pavlopoulou, G. and Dimitriou, D. (2019) '"I don't live with autism; I live with my sister". Sisters' accounts on growing up with their preverbal autistic siblings.' *Research in Developmental Disabilities 88*, 1–15.

24 Pavlopoulou and Dimitriou (n xxx), p.3.

25 Pavlopoulou and Dimitriou (n xxx), p.7.

26 Pavlopoulou and Dimitriou (n xxx), p.7.

27 Tozer, R. and Atkin, K. (2015). '"Recognized, valued and supported"? The experiences of adult siblings of people with autism plus learning disability.' *Journal of Applied Research in Intellectual Disabilities 28*, 4, 341–351, p.231.

28 Ryan, S. (2005) '"Busy behaviour" in the "land of the golden M": Going out with learning disabled children in public places.' *Journal of Applied Research in Intellectual Disabilities 18*, 1, 65–74.

29 Featherstone, H. (1980) *A Difference in the Family: Life with a Disabled Child*. New York, NY: Basic Books, p.57.

Chapter 5

1 Kittay, E. (1999) *Love's Labour: Essays on Women, Equality, and Dependency*. New York, NY: Routledge.

2 Ruddick, S. (1980) 'Maternal thinking.' *Feminist Studies 6*, 2, 342–367.

3 Ryan, S. and Runswick-Cole, K. (2008) 'Repositioning mothers: Mothers, disabled children and disability studies.' *Disability and Society 23*, 3, 199–210.

4 Maich, K., Davies, A.W.J. and Sohrabi, T. (2019) 'Autism spectrum disorder and maternal employment barriers: A comprehensive gender-based enquiry.' *Canadian Journal of Family and Youth 11*, 1, 104–135.

5 Sloper, F.P. and Beresford, B. (2006) 'Families with disabled children.' *BMJ 333*, 928–929.

6 Emerson, E., Hatton, C., Llewellyn, G., Blacker, J. and Graham, H. (2006) 'Socio-economic position, household composition, health status and indicators of well-

being of mothers with and without intellectual disabilities.' *Journal of Intellectual Disability Research 50*, 12, 862–873.

7   Ryan, S. and Runswick Cole, K.R. (2009) 'From advocate to activist? Mapping the experiences of mothers of children on the autism spectrum.' *Journal of Applied Research in Intellectual Disabilities 22*, 1, 43–53.

8   Ryan, S. and Runswick Cole, K.R. (2009) 'From advocate to activist? Mapping the experiences of mothers of children on the autism spectrum.' *Journal of Applied Research in Intellectual Disabilities 22*, 1, 50.

9   Kittay (n xxx), p.181.

Chapter 6

1   Local Government Association/ADASS/NHS England (2015) 'Building the right support: A national plan to develop community services and close inpatient facilities for people with a learning disability and/or autism who display behaviour that challenges, including those with a mental health condition.' Accessed on 12/10/2020 at www.england.nhs.uk/wp-content/uploads/2015/10/ld-nat-imp-plan-oct15.pdf

2   Hall, E. (2009) 'Being in control: Personal budgets and the new landscape of care for people with learning disabilities.' *Mental Health Review Journal 14*, 2, 44–53.

3   BBC (2019) *File on 4: No Place Like Home – The Inside Story of Supported Living.* Released on 12 February 2019. Accessed on 14/2/2020 at https://www.bbc.co.uk/sounds/play/m0002grh

4   The Association of Quality Checkers (AQC) (n.d.) 'Reach: Support for living an ordinary life.' Accessed on 12/2/2020 at http://qualitycheckers.org.uk/about-aqc/quality-checking-tools/the-reach-standards

5   James, E., Harvey, M. and Mitchell, R. (2018) 'An inquiry by social workers into evening routines in community living settings for adults with learning disabilities.' *Practice 30*, 1, 19–32.

6   James, E., Harvey, M. and Mitchell, R. (n.d.) 'An inquiry by social workers into evening routines in community living settings for adults with learning disabilities.' Accessed on 23/2/2020 at https://eprints.lancs.ac.uk/id/eprint/86722/2/Main_Document_Final_Version_After_Feedback_full_author_details_and_affiliations_A_Social_Work_Inqury.pdf, p.13.

7   James, Harvey and Mitchell (n.d.) (n xxx), p.13.

8   Care Quality Commission (n.d.) 'What we do.' Accessed on 12/2/2020 at www.cqc.org.uk/what-we-do

9   Care Standards Tribunal between Care Management Group Ltd and Quality Care Commission: Amended Decision and Reasons (2016). Accessed on 12/2/2020 at http://carestandards.decisions.tribunals.gov.uk//Judgments/j1431/(FTT)%20Amended%20Decision%2014%20August%202018%20-%20%5B2017%5D%203163.EA.pdf

10 https://www.cqc.org.uk/sites/default/files/20170612_registering_the_right_support_final.pdf

11 http://carestandards.decisions.tribunals.gov.uk//Judgments/j1431/(FTT)%2520Amended%2520Decision%252014%2520August%25202018%2520-%2520%255B2017%255D%25203163.EA.pdf

12 p25 (The Dr Joyce's [expert witness] quote

13 p25 (The Dr Joyce's [expert witness] quote

14 Salman, S. (2017) 'You have to give learning disabled people the opportunity to prove themselves.' *The Guardian*. Accessed on 12/2/2020 at www.theguardian.com/society/2017/aug/23/learning-disabled-people-need-work-opportunities

15   Mack, T. (2001) 'We'll do it our way.' *The Guardian*. Accessed on 23/2/2020 at www.theguardian.com/theguardian/2001/apr/14/weekend7.weekend10

16   Trembath, D., Balandin, S., Stancliffe, R.J. and Togher, L. (2010) 'Employment and volunteering for adults with intellectual disability.' *Journal of Policy and Practice in Intellectual Disabilities 7*, 4, 235–238.

17   Butcher, S. and Wilton, R. (2008) 'Stuck in transition? Exploring the spaces of employment training for youth with intellectual disability.' *Geoforum 39*, 2, 1079–1092.

18   BBC News (2017) 'Rosa Monckton: Let learning disabled work below minimum wage.' Accessed on 12/2/2020 at www.bbc.co.uk/news/uk-39138775

19   Busby, M. (2019) 'Tory candidate defends low pay for people with learning disabilities.' *The Guardian*. Accessed on 12/2/2020 at www.theguardian.com/politics/2019/dec/06/tory-candidate-sally-ann-hart-defends-low-pay-people-learning-disabilities

20   Bates, C., Terry, L. and Popple, K. (2017) 'Partner selection for people with intellectual disabilities.' *Journal of Applied Research in Intellectual Disabilities 30*, 4, 602–611.

21   Simon, R. (2002) *Riding the Bus with My Sister: A True Life Journey*. New York, NY: Grand Central Publishing.

22   Quarmby K. (2011) *Scapegoat: Why Are We Failing Disabled People?* London: Portobello Books.

23   Keyes, D. (1966) *Flowers for Algernon*. New York, NY: Harcourt Brace.

24   Wilkinson, M. (2007) 'Three found guilty of murder.' *Oxford Mail*. Accessed on 12/2/2020 at www.oxfordmail.co.uk/news/1338831.three-found-guilty-of-murder

25   BBC News (2018) 'Highbridge's Mendip House staff "engaged in cruel behaviour".' Accessed on 23/2/2020 at www.bbc.co.uk/news/uk-england-somerset-42974755

26   Quarmby K. (2011) *Scapegoat: Why Are We Failing Disabled People?* London: Portobello Books. p.236

27   Langer, E. (2014) 'Daniel Keyes, author of the classic book "Flowers for Algernon," dies at 86.' *The Washington Post*. Accessed on 12/2/2020 at www.washingtonpost.com/entertainment/books/daniel-keyes-author-of-the-classic-book-flowers-for-algernon-dies-at-86/2014/06/18/646e30d6-f6f4-11e3-a606-946fd632f9f1_story.html

28   Tozer, R. and Atkin, K., (2015). '"Recognized, valued and supported"? The experiences of adult siblings of people with autism plus learning disability.' *Journal of Applied Research in Intellectual Disabilities 28*, 4, 341–351.

29   Rittenour, C.E., Myers, S.A. and Brann, M. (2007) 'Commitment and emotional closeness in the sibling relationship.' *Southern Communication Journal 72*, 2, 169–183.

30   Conway, S. and Meyer, D. (2008) 'Developing support for siblings of young people with disabilities.' *Support for Learning 23*, 113–117.

31   Moss, P., Eirinaki, V., Savage, S. and Howlin, P. (2019) 'Growing older with autism: The experiences of adult siblings of individuals with autism.' *Research in Autism Spectrum Disorders 63*, 42–51.

32   Tozer and Atkin (n xxx).

33   Tozer and Atkin (n xxx), p.237.

34   Power, A. and Bartlett, R. (2019) 'Ageing with a learning disability: Care and support in the context of austerity.' *Social Science and Medicine 231*, 55–61.

35   Buchanan, I. and Walmsley, J. (2006) 'Self-advocacy in historical perspective.' *British Journal of Learning Disabilities 34*, 3, 133–138.

36   Clement T. (2003) 'An ethnography of people first anytown: A description, analysis and interpretation of an organisational culture.' Unpublished PhD thesis, Open University, Milton Keynes.

37   Department of Health and Social Care (2001) *Valuing People: A New Strategy for*

Learning Disability for the 21st Century. Accessed on 23/2/2020 at www.gov.uk/government/publications/valuing-people-a-new-strategy-for-learning-disability-for-the-21st-century

38 Walmsley, J. and Armstrong, A. (2019) 'Making sense of self-advocacy today: Report to RTR.' Accessed on 12/2/2020 at http://pathwaysassociates.co.uk/uploads/media/files/news-downloads/RTR%20Report%2012%20June.pdf

39 http://pathwaysassociates.co.uk/partners/news/making-sense-of-self-advocacy-today.html , p.33.

Chapter 7

1   Power, A. and Bartlett, R. (2019) 'Ageing with a learning disability: Care and support in the context of austerity.' *Social Science and Medicine 231*, 55–61.

2   Grey, J.M., Totsika, V. and Hastings, R.P. (2018) 'Physical and psychological health of family carers co-residing with an adult relative with an intellectual disability.' *Journal of Applied Research in Intellectual Disabilities 31*, 52, 191–202.

3   Digital NHS (2018) *Health and Care of People with Learning Disabilities: 2017–18*. Accessed on 13/2/2020 at https://files.digital.nhs.uk/BA/4F4C1D/health-care-learning-disabilities-1718-sum.pdf

4   O'Dwyer, C., McCallion, P., Henman, M. (2019) 'Prevalence and patterns of antipsychotic use and their associations with mental health and problem behaviours among older adults with intellectual disabilities.' *Journal of Applied Research in Intellectual Disabilities 32*, 4, 981–993.

5   Michael, C. (2016) 'Why we need research about autism and ageing.' *Autism 20*, 5, 515–516, p.516.

6   Heslop, P., Blair, P., Fleming, P., Hoghton, M., Marriott, A. and Russ, L. (2013) *Confidential Inquiry into Premature Deaths of People with Learning Disabilities*. Accessed on 12/2/202 at www.bristol.ac.uk/media-library/sites/cipold/migrated/documents/fullfinalreport.pdf

7   Emerson, E. and Hatton, C. (2013) *Health Inequalities and People with Intellectual Disabilities*. Cambridge: Cambridge University Press.

8   Hatton, C. (2019) Personal communication, 22 March 2019.

9   Deville, J., Davies, H., Kane, R., Nelson, D. and Mansfield, P. (2019) 'Planning for the future: Exploring the experiences of older carers of adult children with a learning disability.' *British Journal of Learning Disabilities 47*, 3, 208–214.

10 Mahon, A., Tilley, E., Randhawa, G., Pappas, Y. and Vseteckova, J. (2019) 'Ageing carers and intellectual disability: A scoping review.' *Quality in Ageing and Older Adults 20*, 4, 162–178.

11 Davys, D. and Haigh, C. (2008) 'Older parents of people who have a learning disability: Perceptions of future accommodation needs.' *British Journal of Learning Disabilities 36*, 1, 66–72.

12 MacHale, R. and Carey, S. (2002) 'An investigation of the effects of bereavement on mental health and challenging behaviour in adults with learning disability.' *British Journal of Learning Disabilities 30*, 3, 113–117.

13 Ledger, S. (2012) 'Staying Local.' Unpublished PhD thesis, Open University, Milton Keynes.

14 Deville, J., Davies, H., Kane, R., Nelson, D. and Mansfield, P. (2019) 'Planning for the future: Exploring the experiences of older carers of adult children with a learning disability.' *British Journal of Learning Disabilities 47*, 3, 208–214.

15 Bibby, R. (2012) '"I hope he goes first": Exploring determinants of engagement in future planning for adults with a learning disability living with ageing parents.

What are the issues? A literature review.' *British Journal of Learning Disabilities 41*, 2, 94–105.

16 National Institute for Health and Care Excellence (2018) 'Care and support of people growing older with learning disabilities. NICE guideline [NG96].' Accessed on 12/2/2020 at www.nice.org.uk/guidance/ng96/chapter/Recommendations

17 Furniss, K.A., Loverseed, A., Lippold, T. and Dodd, K. (2012) 'The views of people who care for adults with Down's syndrome and dementia: A service evaluation.' *British Journal of Learning Disabilities 40*, 4, 318–427.

18 Furniss *et al.* (n xxx).

19 Power, A. and Bartlett, R. (2019) 'Ageing with a learning disability: Care and support in the context of austerity.' *Social Science and Medicine 231*, 55–61.

20 Power and Bartlett (n xxx).

21 DeVerteuil, G. (2015) *Resilience in the Post-Welfare Inner City*. Bristol: Policy Press, p.6.

22 Get the Picture (2017) 'What will happen when I am no longer around?' Accessed on 12/2/2020 at www.youtube.com/watch?v=AMvbrhA2nUk

23 Ryan, S. (2018) 'Honouring a life and narrative work: John's story.' *Arts and Humanities in Higher Education 17*, 1, 58–68.

24 Vogel, J.S. (2018) *A Mythopoetic Exploration of Maternal Grief: When a Child is Diagnosed on the Autism Spectrum*. Carpenteria, CA: Pacifica Graduate Institute.

25 Tuffrey-Wijne, I., Bernal, J., Hubert, J., Butler, G. and Hollins, S. (2010) 'Exploring the lived experiences of people with learning disabilities who are dying of cancer.' *Nursing Times 106*, 19, 15–18; Tuffrey-Wijne, I., Giatras, N., Butler, G., Cresswell, A., Manners, P. and Bernal, J. (2013) 'Developing guidelines for disclosure or non-disclosure of bad news around life-limiting illness and death to people with intellectual disabilities.' *Journal of Applied Research in Intellectual Disabilities 26*, 3, 231–242.

26 McRitchie, R., McKenzie, K., Quayle, E., Harlin, M. and Neumann, K. (2014) 'How adults with an intellectual disability experience bereavement and grief: A qualitative exploration.' *Death Studies 38*, 3, 179–185.

27 McRitchie *et al.* (n xxx).

28 Hollins, S., Blackman, N. and Dowling, S. (2003) *When Somebody Dies* (Books Beyond Words). London: Gaskell.

29 Glover, G., Williams, R., Heslop, P., Oyinlola, J. and Grey, J. (2017) 'Mortality in people with intellectual disabilities in England.' *Journal of Intellectual Disability Research 61*, 1, 62–74.

30 Michael, J. (2008) *Healthcare for All: Report of the Independent Inquiry into Access to Healthcare for People with Learning Disabilities*. Accessed on 13/2/2020 at https://webarchive.nationalarchives.gov.uk/20130105064250/http://www.dh.gov.uk/en/Publicationsandstatistics/Publications/PublicationsPolicyAndGuidance/DH_099255

31 Haveman, M., Perry, J., Salvador-Carulla, L., Walsh, P.N. *et al.* (2011) 'Ageing and health status in adults with intellectual disabilities: Results of the European POMONA II study.' *Journal of Intellectual and Developmental Disability 36*, 1, 49–60.

32 Norah Fry Centre for Disability Studies (2017) 'Learning Disabilities Mortality Review (LeDeR).' Accessed on 10/2/2020 at www.bristol.ac.uk/sps/leder

33 Tuffrey-Wijne, I. and Davidson, J. (2018) 'Excellence in palliative and end-of-life care provision for people with intellectual disability.' *International Journal of Palliative Nursing 24*, 12, 598–610.

34 Tuffrey-Wijne, I., Wicki, M., Heslop, P., McCarron, M. *et al.* (2016) 'Developing research priorities for palliative care of people with intellectual disabilities in Europe: A consultation process using nominal group technique.' *BMC Palliative Care*

15, 36; Tuffrey-Wijne, I., Todd, S., Hatton, C., Glover, G. *et al.* (2019) 'A theoretical framework of the factors affecting the end-of-life (EOL) trajectory and provision of end-of-life care (EOLC) for people with intellectual disabilities (ID).' International Association for the Scientific Study of Intellectual and Developmental Disabilities World Congress.

35 Vrijmoeth, C., Barten, P., Assendelft, W.J.J., Christians, M.G.M. *et al.* (2016) 'Physicians' identification of the need for palliative care in people with intellectual disabilities.' *Research in Developmental Disabilities 59*, 55–64; Vrijmoeth, C., Christians, M.G., Festen, D.A., Groot, M. *et al.* (2016) 'Physician-reported symptoms and interventions in people with intellectual disabilities approaching end of life.' *Journal of Palliative Medicine 19*, 11, 1142–1147.

36 Dunkley, S. and Sales, R. (2014) 'The challenges of providing palliative care for people with intellectual disabilities: A literature review.' *International Journal of Palliative Nursing 20*, 6, 279–284.

37 Tuffrey-Wijne, I., Giatras, N., Butler, G., Cresswell, A., Manners, P. and Bernal, J. (2013) 'Developing guidelines for disclosure or non-disclosure of bad news around life-limiting illness and death to people with intellectual disabilities.' *Journal of Applied Research in Intellectual Disabilities 26*, 3, 231–242.

38 Webber, R., Bowers, B. and Bigby, C. (2010) 'Hospital experiences of older people with intellectual disability: Responses of group home staff and family members.' *Journal of Intellectual and Developmental Disability 35*, 3, 155–164.

39 Tuffrey-Wijne, I., Bernal, J., Hubert, J., Butler, G. and Hollins, S. (2009) 'People with learning disabilities who have cancer: An ethnographic study.' *British Journal of General Practice 59*, 564, 503–509.

40 Watchman K. (2005) 'Practitioner-raised issues and end-of-life care for adults with Down syndrome and dementia.' *Journal of Policy and Practice in Intellectual Disabilities 2*, 2, 156–162.

41 BBC News (2019) 'Giuseppe Ulleri inquest: Hospital's feeding failure "led to death".' Accessed on 13/2/2020 at www.bbc.co.uk/news/uk-england-manchester-47751095

42 City and Hackney Safeguarding Adults Board (2019) 'Safeguarding Adult Review into Death of JoJo.' Accessed on 11/2/2020 at http://files.localgov.co.uk/jojo-sar.pdf

43 City and Hackney Safeguarding Adults Board (n xxx), p.46.

44 Sheridan, E. (2019) 'Death of woman with Down's syndrome from scabies could have been avoided, report finds.' *Hackney Citizen*. Accessed on 23/2/2020 at www.hackneycitizen.co.uk/2019/07/25/death-woman-downs-syndrome-scabies-avoided-safeguarding

Chapter 8

1 https://www.england.nhs.uk/publication/learning-from-deaths-guidance-for-nhs-trusts-on-working-with-bereaved-families-and-carers

Chapter 8

2 Kittay, E. (1999) *Love's Labour: Essays on Women, Equality, and Dependency.* New York, NY: Routledge, p.178.

3 Runswick-Cole, K. and Ryan, S. (2019) 'Liminal still? Unmothering disabled children.' *Disability and Society 34*, 7–8, 1125–1139.

Subject Index

1800 Seconds of Autism
  (podcast) 22–3

Aabe, Nura 74
acronym use 86–7
activism 106–10
Adult Training
  Facilities 124
adulthood
  lack of services in 113–5
  see also independent
    supported living;
    transitions
advocacy
  parent 106–10
  self- 133–6
antidepressant use 103
antipsychotic medication
  137–8
apologising for behaviour 83
Applied Behavioural
  Analysis (ABA) 73
Asperger, Hans 37
Asperger's syndrome 37–8
Assisted Loving (radio
  programme) 126–7
austerity politics 91,
  115, 140
autism
  Asperger's syndrome
    37–8
  'discovery' of 37
  'triad of impairments' 38
  UK community 38
Autism Act (2009) 38
Autism Independence 74

babies/toddlers
  developmental milestones
    49–53, 63
  early signs of
    difference 47–8
  'good' babies 50–1
  missed milestones
    49–53, 63
  unusual vocal patterns
    49–50
  vague feelings about
    difference 51–2
Bates, Clare 126, 127
Baxter, Otto 134–5
bedtimes (early) 119, 125–6
bereavement/grief 150
Big Bedtime Audit 119
Breaking Point campaign 43
#BrewEd events 24–5
Bryan, Terry 39
'Building the Right Support'
  programme 114
bureaucracy 100–1
bystander inaction 128

Care Quality Commission
  Cherry Tree hearing
    119–22
  creation of 32
  inspections 122
Caring for People White
  Paper (1989) 35
categorization/labelling 30–2
censure (public) 81–3
Challenging Behaviours
  (podcast) 129–30

Charity for the Asylum
  of Idiots 30
Cherry Tree/CQC
  hearing 119–22
Children in Need 19
co-mingling 24
community care, shift to 35
Confidential Inquiry into the
  Premature Deaths of
  People with Learning
  Disabilities (CIPOLD)
  (2013) 36, 43
cultural differences 74–5

Death by Indifference
  report (2007) 35
deaths
  in independent supported
    living 117–8
  of main caregiver 139
  National Mortality
    Review Board 36
  premature 35–6, 44
deficit model 19, 67
dependency work
  overview 68, 95–6
  paid employment
    and 96–8
  tasks of 98–9
developmental milestones
  49–53, 63
diagnosis
  associations of word 48
  as a beginning 58–9
  being told 56–61, 64
  in childhood 49–56

diagnosis *cont.*
Connor's 62–5
delay in getting 53–4
deliberately undiagnosed
children 48
experiences of
getting 53–6
information given at 61–2
late in adulthood 146–9
responses to 57–61
route to 54–6
disability movement 35
Disability Studies field 96
disablism 17–8
double empathy problem 38

education
Education Act (1981) 33
Education (Handicapped
Children) Act
(1970) 33
Education Health
and Care (EHC)
plans 114
Education and Support
Allowance 75, 100–1
'insane' arguments from
school 71–3
Edwards, Michael
124, 133–4
Ely Hospital scandal 32
Embolden project 141–6
employment
Adult Training
Facilities 124
and dependency
work 96–8
opportunities for 123–5
paid 125
volunteering 124–5
end-of-life care 150–3
Equality Act (2010) 41
ethnic minority groups 74–5
Eugenics Education
Society 30
eugenics movement 31
experience of disability
(previous) 22

'familiar others' 22
Flowers for Algernon
(book) 128–9
form-filling 100–1
Foxes Academy 124

friendships 126
Fulfilling and Rewarding
Lives (2011) 38
fun 125–6
future
planning for 138–40
worrying about 105,
113, 139
see also adulthood

Gallagher, Caoilfhionn 13
Galton, Francis 31
'gifted child' behaviours 52
Gig Buddies 126
going out in public 80–4
good practice examples
24–6, 84, 88–91,
110–1, 157–4
GPs dismissing concerns 54
grief/bereavement 150
guilt (mothers') 101–2

Hanrahan, Gail 75, 97
Hartley, Edward 44
health and wellbeing
older learning-disabled
people 137–8
parents 102–4
hospitals (long-stay) 32–5
human rights approach 41

Idiots Act (1886) 30
inclusion phobia 21, 26,
41, 48, 128, 156
independent supported living
Cherry Tree/CQC
hearing 119–22
funding for 118–9
good examples 122–3
overview 117–9
staff shortages 118–9
individual budgets 35, 116–7
industrialization age 29
information
finding useable 74–5
given at diagnosis 61–2
inquests
Connor 44
Edward Hartley 44
Henry 44–5
inconsistencies at 45

'insane' behaviour/advice
professionals 71–3,
91–2, 121
schools 71–3
institutionalization
history of 30–2
long-stay hospitals 32–5
'intelligence' (concept of) 31

jargon use 86–7
#JusticeforLB campaign
13–5

Knight, Jayne 118
knowledge
professional and personal
overlap 70–3
self-education 24, 69

labelling/categorization 30–2
language use (professionals')
86–7
LeDeR reviews 36
legislation see policy/
legislation
life expectancy
increases 138–9
long-stay hospitals 32–5
love, recognizing 26–7

marginalization 18–20, 74–5
Mazars review (2015) 44
meetings with professionals
84–91
Mencap 32–3
Mental Deficiency
Act (1913) 31
Michael, Cos 137
missed milestones 49–53, 63
moral pioneers 73
mother blame 37, 102
see also parents
'Mum' (being addressed
as) 87
My Life My Choice
group 133–5

National Mortality
Review Board 36
Neary, Mark 117
neurodiversity 38
Nicholson, David 44

No Place Like Home (radio programme) 117–9
normalization activity 23
normative beliefs 23

Oxfordshire Family Support Network (OxFSN) 75, 97, 141

parents
    death of main caregiver 139
    getting older 130–1, 141–6
    guilt/self-blame 101–2
    health and wellbeing 102–4
    as moral pioneers 73
    mother blame 37, 102
    not listened to 54, 72
    single-parent households 68, 104
    typically women's work 95
    see also dependency work; knowledge
personal budgets 35, 116–7
podcasts
    1800 Seconds of Autism 22–3
    Challenging Behaviours 129–30
policy/legislation
    Autism Act (2009) 38
    Caring for People White Paper (1989) 35
    Education Act (1981) 33
    Education (Handicapped Children) Act (1970) 33
    Equality Act (2010) 41
    human rights approach 41
    Idiots Act (1886) 30
    Mental Deficiency Act (1913) 31
    UN Convention on the Rights of Persons with Disabilities (2006) 41
    Valuing People (2001) 35
    Valuing People Now (2009) 35

professionals
    appointments with 84–91
    definition of 16
    good practice examples 24–6, 84, 88–91, 110–1, 157–4
    'insane' behaviour by 71–3, 91–2, 121
    public, going out in 80–4

Raphael, Christian 123
Reach standards 118
'refrigerator mothers' 37
relationships
    friendships 126
    marital 104
    sexual 126–7
    sibling 75–80
Riding the Bus with My Sister (book) 127
Royal Earlswood Hospital 30
'rule-breaking' in public 81
Runswick-Cole, Katherine 25–6

Scapegoat (book) 127–8
schools see education
self-advocacy 133–6
self-blame (mothers') 101–2
self-education 24, 69
sexual relationships 126–7
Shaw, George Bernard 30
siblings
    in adulthood 131–3
    framing of research findings 76–80, 131
    moving on/leaving home 115
    research into experiences of 75–80
Silent Minority documentary 33–5, 42, 156
single-parent households 68, 104
Smith, Isobel 130–1
social enterprise cafés 124
social media platforms 109
South Asian communities 74
'sparkling tweets' 24–6, 84, 88–91, 110–1, 157–4
Spectrum of Obstacles report (2016) 38–9

Stay Up Late charity 125–6
stigma 21
Sunman, Jan 97
support, assumption of 60
support groups 24, 106–10
supported living see independent supported living
sympathetic others 21–2

Tang, Sui-Ling 126–7
Think Autism (2014) 38
transitions
    concept of 113
    Connor and 115–6
    current situation 116–7
    see also adulthood
'triad of impairments' 38

UN Convention on the Rights of Persons with Disabilities (2006) 41
Undateables (tv programme) 126
University College London 31–2

Valuing People (2001) 35
Valuing People Now (2009) 35
volunteering 124–5

'Walk it like you talk it' campaign 125
wellbeing (parents') 102–4
Wells, H.G. 30
Westminster Commission on Autism 38
Wiltshire, Dawn 134
Winterbourne View scandal 39–40
'wise', becoming 23–4
Woolf, Virginia 30
work see employment

Yellow Submarine charity 124
Young, Toby 31

Author Index

Abbott, D. 16*n6*
ADASS 40*n28*, 114*n1*
Ali, Z. 74*n15*
Armstrong, A. 135*n38*
Association of Quality
    Checkers 118*n4*
Atkin, K. 77*n27*, 131*n28*,
    132*n32*, 132*n33*
Avery, D. 67*n1*

Bartlett, R. 133*n34*, 137*n1*,
    140*n19*, 141*n20*
Bates, C. 126*n20*
Bates, K. 16*n4*
BBC News 117*n3*, 125*n18*,
    128*n5*, 152*n44*
Beresford, B. 102*n5*
Bettelheim, B. 37*n22*
Bibby, R. 140*n15*
Bigby, C. 151*n38*
Blackburn, C. 68*n4*
Blackman, N. 150*n28*
Booth, R. 41*n31*
Boshoff, K. 53*n2*
Bowers, B. 151*n38*
Brann, M. 131*n29*
Broach, S. 68*n5*, 68*n6*
Buchanan, I. 133*n35*
Burns, J. 16*n6*
Busby, M. 125*n19*
Butcher, S. 125*n17*

Care Quality Commission
    119*n8*
Carey, S. 139*n12*

City and Hackney
    Safeguarding Adults
    Board 70*n8*, 152*n42*
Clement T. 133*n36*
Clements, L. 41*n30*,
    68*n5*, 68*n6*, 74*n13*
Cole, S. 75*n19*
Connolly, K. 37*n18*
Connors, C. 76*n22*
Conway, S. 131*n30*
Cook, B. 24*n6*
Crane, L. 48*n1*, 53*n2*,
    53*n5*, 60*n5*

Davidson, J. 151n33
Davies, A.W.J. 96*n4*
Davys, D. 139*n11*
Department for Business,
    Innovation and
    Skills 38*n26*
Department for
    Education 38*n26*
Department of Health
    35*n9*, 35*n13*
Department of Health and
    Social Care 35*n10*,
    38*n26*, 38*n25*, 135*n37*
Department for
    Transport 38*n26*
Department for Work and
    Pensions 38*n26*
DeVerteuil, G. 141*n21*
Deville, J. 139*n14*, 139*n9*
Digby, A. 29*n1*
Digital NHS 137*n3*
Dimitriou, D. 22*n4*, 76*n23*,
    76*n24*, 77*n25*, 77*n26*
Dowling, S. 150*n28*

Dunkley, S. 151*n36*

Emerson, E. 103*n6*, 137*n7*

Featherstone, H.
    17*n8*, 92*n29*
Ferraioli, S.J. 76*n20*
Fox, F. 74*n17*, 74*n18*
Furniss, K.A. 140*n17*,
    140*n18*

Garnett, M. 24*n6*
Get the Picture 141*n22*
Glover, G. 150*n29*
Goffman, E. 21*n2*, 22*n3*
Goodey, C.F. 21*n1*
Goodley, D. 16*n4*, 18*n9*
Grey, J.M. 137*n2*
Guardian 36*n15*

Haigh, C. 139*n11*
Hall, E. 116*n2*
Hammond, L. 75*n19*
Harris, S.L. 76*n20*
Harvey, M. 119*n5*,
    119*n6*, 119*n7*
Hastings, R.P. 137*n2*
Hatton, C. 16*n2*, 68*n3*,
    74*n14*, 138*n7*, 139*n8*
Haveman, M. 151*n31*
Henman, M. 138*n4*
Heslop, P. 36*n14*, 138*n6*
Hevey, D. 19*n10*
Hewitson, J. 22*n5*
Hirvikoski, T. 36*n17*
Hollins, S. 150*n28*

James, E. 119n5,
119n6, 119n7
James, L. 24n7

Kanner, L. 37n19, 37n20
Keyes, D. 127n23
Kim, C. 24n8
King's Fund 33n8
Kittay, E. 68n2, 70n7,
95n1, 111n9, 156n2

Langer, E. 129n27
Learning Disability
Mortality Review 16n3
Ledger, S. 139n13
Lehmann-Haupt, C. 37n21
Liasidou, A. 74n16
Local Government
Association
40n28, 114n1
Lomas, C. 40n29
Lovell, B. 76n21

McCallion, P. 138n4
McFadden, J. 30n3
MacHale, R. 139n12
Mack, T. 124n15
McRitchie, R. 150n26,
151n27
McVilly, K.R. 16n5
Mahon, A. 139n10
Maich, K. 96n4
Mencap 35n11, 43n33
Meyer, D. 131n30
Michael, C. 138n5
Michael, J. 35n12, 151n30
Milton, D. 38n24, 73n11
Ministry of Justice 38n26
Mitchell, R. 119n5,
119n6, 119n7
Mitchell, W. 74n12
Morris, P. 32n6, 33n7

Moss, P. 131n31
Munroe, K. 75n19
Myers, S.A. 131n29

National Institute for
Health and Care
Excellence 140n16
NHS England 40n28, 114n1
Norah Fry Centre for
Disability Studies
36n16, 151n32

O'Dwyer, C. 138n4

Pavlopoulou, G. 22n4,
76n23, 76n24,
77n25, 77n26
People's Collection
Wales 32n5
Popple, K. 126n20
Power, A. 133n34, 137n1,
140n19, 141n20
Pring, J. 41n32

Quality Care Commission
120n9
Quarmby K. 127n22, 128n26

Rapp, R. 73n9
Raw, L. 31n4
Read, J. 41n30, 68n4, 74n13
Reinders, J.S. 16n7
Rittenour, C.E. 131n29
Ruddick, S. 95n2
Runswick Cole, K.R.
16n4, 96n3, 108n7,
109n8, 157n3
Ryan, S. 13n1, 54n4, 61n6,
80n28, 96n3, 108n7,
109n8, 146n23, 157n3

Sales, R. 151n36
Salisbury, H. 54n4, 61n6
Salman, S. 124n14
Sheridan, E. 153n44
Silberman, S. 29n2
Silverman, C. 26n9, 73n10
Simon, R. 127n21
Sloper, F.P. 102n5
Sloper, P. 74n12
Sohrabi, T. 96n4
Spencer, N. 68n4
Stalker, K. 76n22

Terry, L. 126n20
Totsika, V. 137n2
Tozer, R. 77n27, 131n28,
132n32, 132n33
Trembath, D. 124n16
Tuffrey-Wijne, I. 150n25,
151n33, 151n34,
151n37, 151n39

Vogel, J.S. 150n24
Vrijmoeth, C. 151n35

Walmsley, J. 133n35, 135n38
Watchman K. 152n40
Webber, R. 151n38
Westminster Commission
on Autism 38n27
Wetherell, M.A. 76n21
Wilkinson, M. 128n24
Wilton, R. 125n17
Wing, L. 38n23
Wright, D. 29n1

Printed in Great Britain
by Amazon

50435357R00106